Maritime Fleetwood

A Photographic Record

by Alan Hirst & Peter Horsley

Hutton Press
1996

Published by

The Hutton Press Ltd.,
130 Canada Drive, Cherry Burton,
Beverley, East Yorkshire HU17 7SB

Copyright © 1996

Printed by
Image Colourprint Ltd.,
Grange Park Lane,
Willerby, Hull
HU10 6EB

ISBN 1 872167 85 3

Contents

Acknowledgements

Most of the photographs used in the compiling of this book are original photographs by Peter Horsley. Some of the illustrations are from the Peter Horsley Collection and photographs kindly supplied by others have been individualy credited. We are most grateful for the ready help and assistance we have had from so many people and special thanks must go to ...

Arthur Airey, John Bamforth, Ian Baxter, Fred Bettess, Alan Blundell, David Buckley, Norman Bullen, Evelyn Chantler, William Chard, Harold Colley, Ron Cox, Cyril Head, Tony Lofthouse, Colin Lynch, John Noble, Alec Slater, Alan Taylor and Jack Worthington.

Also to ...

I.C.I. Limited, Lancashire County Council staff at Fleetwood Library, Fleetwood Museum, and the Lancashire Record Office, Preston.

Chapter 1

Cargo Traffic Through Fleetwood

The river Wyre was a well used waterway long before the port of Fleetwood was conceived in the 1830's. At Poulton-le-Fylde ("Pool town") just a few miles up-river from the present-day Wyre Dock, the Blackburne family were well established merchant traders who before 1600 were recorded as importing flax and tallow from Russia. In 1688, Richard Parke of Poulton was recorded as joint owner of a vessel *Samaritan of Wyre*. Poulton was a subsidiary port under Chester prior to 1700, had a Custom House built before 1708 and became a sub-port under Lancaster. A wharf and warehouse were built at Wardleys and at Skippool a warehouse was built in 1741 for trade with Barbados. Records of 1742 list this West Indies trade as including sugar, rum and cotton. Customs records at Poulton record later imports which include timber from Russia and America, guano (nitrates) from West Africa and also wine, tea and tobacco. Flax remained a significant import, the warehouses at Wardleys serving the linen and sailcloth mills at nearby Kirkham whilst Poulton, too, had sailcloth manufacturing. Most of the vessels working into the old port of Poulton-le-Fylde in the years up to the building of Fleetwood would be engaged in coastwise trade to West Coast ports such as Liverpool, Lancaster and Whitehaven and would include sailing flats, sloops and ketches. *Lovely Sea* was a sailing flat built at Preston in 1813 and jointly owned by Richard Shepherd of Preesall and Jeremiah Parkinson of Pilling. The *Trafalgar* was a sloop built in 1836 for Thomas Seed of Poulton-le-Fylde. Some larger ships were owned by local men. The *Harriet* built at Lytham in 1824 was a two-masted schooner owned by Robert Bibby and *Content* was a Brigantine owned by the Knowles brothers, local merchants at Poulton. The only large vessel known to have been built locally during this period was the three-masted barque *Hope* built at Wardleys in 1836 and engaged in the timber trade.

As Fleetwood's harbour facilities became available in the late 1830's this traffic was transferred to the new port, as was the Custom House when Fleetwood became a "Distinct Port" in 1839. Fleetwood had the advantage of the Preston and Wyre Railway, opened in 1840, which not only continued the trade to Poulton and Kirkham but by connecting with other railways could serve a much wider of Lancashire and its expanding industries and rapidly growing towns. In 1846 records show 823 ship movements bringing 144,622 tons of cargo to Fleetwood. The port's enclosed dock was not built until 1877 but in the years prior to the opening of the Wyre Dock Fleetwood's riverside quays served an increasing overseas and coastal trade. The steamers on the Fleetwood - Belfast service, which started in 1843, were all built to carry cargo as well as passengers and in addition to this continuous Irish traffic large sailing ships brought timber, grain, cotton and tobacco to the port. Large numbers of smaller ships - schooners, brigs, ketches and flats as well as steamers working coastal and short-sea routes brought to Fleetwood slate from Wales, china-clay from Cornwall, timber from the Baltic, wine from Portugal and iron from Scotland and across Morecambe Bay from Furness and Cumbria. Fleetwood's principal export activity in the 1800's was the shipping of coal, mostly to Ireland, a trade which increased from 1869 onwards when several steam-ships began to be employed in the trade.

The opening of Wyre Dock in 1877 saw a rapid rise in trade. Timber, grain, cotton, pig-iron and iron ore remained the chief imports but the volume handled greatly increased. Outward trade from Fleetwood to foreign ports failed to expand, most large ships went to other ports for export cargoes. At first, Fleetwood was a very attractive port for shipping companies to use.

As a railway owned port, goods forwarded by rail carried low charges and the port had a marked cost advantage over Liverpool. The port's Grain Elevator came into use in 1883 and by 1885 grain and timber imports together with cotton, iron ore, pig-iron, esperato-fibre, wood pulp and general cargo took the port to full-stretch. Ships often had to wait at anchor in the Lune Deeps of Morecambe Bay because the dock was full. By 1890, apart from the Railway owned Belfast steamers, Fleetwood's own shipping companies owned and operated from the port, 3 barques, 34 two and three masted schooners, a single-screw steamship *Thursby* of 497 gross tons, and numerous small trading ketches and sloops. The number of cargo ships using Fleetwood peaked, however, in 1894. New docks at Preston had syphoned off some of Fleetwood's trade and when the Manchester Ship Canal opened in 1894, making Manchester and Salford seaports in the heartland of Lancashire's industrial region, Fleetwood's cargo trade went into deep decline.

Fortunately for the continuance of the dock, from the beginning of the 20th Century, whilst cargo traffic to Wyre Dock fell to relative insignificance the port's Fishing Industry expanded rapidly. A jetty at Preesall, across the river from Wyre Dock, had been built in 1893 to serve the Salt mines being exploited there and in 1894 a private jetty was opened at Burn Naze, just upriver from Wyre Dock, to serve the United Alkali Company works. Rock-salt was exported from the Preesall jetty and Soda Ash, pure Salt and alkaline products went out from Burn Naze. Limestone was brought to the Burn Naze jetty from quarries in North Wales. Though Fleetwood's docks were largely taken over by the trawler fleets some cargo traffic continued - mainly much reduced quantities of timber, parcels of boards for fish-boxes, barrel staves, some China clay, cement, potatoes and occasional general cargoes. Export traffic seems largely to have been shipments of gravel, fish products such as salt-cod and casual consignments to other U.K. ports.

The post-war years since 1945 have seen another rise and fall in Fleetwood's cargo trade. The I.C.I. works at Burn Naze grew into a chemicals complex which produced PVC plastics, Alkathene, Fluon, Polyurethane, Phosgene, Nylon and much more. At various times basic chemical shipments have been brought to or shipped out of Wyre Dock for I.C.I. Limited. Oil and diesel fuel came to the port as the fishing fleet changed from coal-fired steam trawlers to motor trawlers. Fruit and vegetable shipments from Spain, Cyprus and Egypt came quite regularly to Fleetwood and in 1968 timber imports resumed. The 1970's saw the large scale exporting of scrap metal begin and the re-establishment of Fleetwood as a grain port, the two trades complementing each other in as much as ships bringing grain to the port often sailed out with a cargo of scrap.

All these ventures prospered for some years but by 1989 they had all died out as the pattern of trading within the Common Market shifted to the East coast and as road-hauled containerised loads became the norm and made use of the Ro-Ro ferries. Wyre Dock became a yachting marina. Nevertheless, Fleetwood's Roll-on/roll-off Link-span berth, opened in 1975 on the site of the port's original riverside quays of the 1840's, handles a greater annual volume of trade than that which passed through the port in the days of sailing ships and steamers.

Sailing ships moored in the "Canshe Hole", a natural deep-water basin in the River Wyre which enabled vessels to remain afloat even at low water. A photograph believed to date from about 1875.

A single masted sloop rigged 'Flat'.

The sailing 'Flat' here seen sitting squarely on the bank on the East side of the Wyre Dock channel illustrates exactly how these vessels were built to trade into the tidal creeks around the coast. At low tide they would safely take the ground and would often off-load directly into horse drawn carts where these could be brought alongside the ship. The little vessel pictured here in 1881 was built and would have been operated in exactly the same manner as the first vessels to land at Fleetwood their cargoes of stone, timber, slates, ironwork, cement and the like needed in the building of the town and its quays. Sir Peter Hesketh-Fleetwood had ten single-masted sailing flats built for service during the building of his town and port. In 1837 the flats *Fleetwood* and *Hesketh* were built at Lytham and *Breeze* and *Daring* were built at Preston. The other vessels were added in 1838, *Atlas*, *Arthur*, *Owen* and *Colonel* were built at Fleetwood whilst *Witch* and *Blazer* came from the yard at Glasson Dock. *Atlas*, *Blazer*, *Owen* and *Witch* were later bought by the railway company and, dismasted, were converted for use as lighters.

A crowd of sailing vessels in Wyre Dock, a photograph thought to be one of the earliest pictures taken on Fleetwood's dock which was opened in 1877.

A four-masted barque at Fleetwood.

Many three and four masted vessels, barques and others fully square rigged on all masts, brought cargoes to Fleetwood between 1877 and the years of the 1914-1918 War. Included in the lists of vessels at Fleetwood were some of the most notable "Tall-ships" from the last days of deep-water sail. *Kenilworth*, *Holt Hill*, *Falls of Clyde*, *Royal Forth*, *Port Stanley*, *Gifford*, *Kinrosshire*, *Drummuir*, *Lawhill*, and many more appear in the Fleetwood dock-traffic record. The largest single grain shipload ever to be brought into the port by a sailing ship was recorded in May, 1905 when the German four-mast barque *Adelaide* (ex *Holken* built in 1888 for Liverpool owners) brought 4700 tons of wheat from San Francisco.

Invercauld.

The three-mast, steel hulled, Aberdeen barque *Invercauld* was another "Tall ship" which brought cargo to Fleetwood. An earlier *Invercauld*, a full-rigged ship, was wrecked on the Aukland Islands south-east of New Zealand in 1865. Her successor was built by McMillan & Son at Dumbarton in 1891 and was photograped here taking grain to the Solway Mills at Silloth. *Invercauld's* Master was Australian born Captain A.G.F. Kebblewhite and at Fleetwood he met and married local girl Millicent Gerrard. His young wife accompanied her husband on his voyages, as was commonly done then, and he taught her to steer the ship, how to use a sextant and to navigate. When he retired the couple returned to Fleetwood where the Captain died in 1927. Seaside born and a member of a seafaring family, the Captain's widow returned to sea, she became a Stewardess with the Cunard White Star Line. *Photo. courtesy of John Noble.*

Sailing out light after discharging at Fleetwood.

Most of the large sailing vessels which brought cargoes to Fleetwood appear to have left the port light after discharging their cargo and went to other ports to pick up another. Here, in this photograph from an original glass-plate negative in the Peter Horsley collection and thought to date from about 1900, a barquentine is making sail. The vessel is light, apparently having little or no ballast, and would probably have been towed out to the Lune Deeps by one of Fleetwood's tugs prior to making the short run to one of the Mersey docks.

Sail and Steam in Wyre Dock.

The Grimsby steam trawler *New Crown* seen here was built by Earles at Hull and then landed her maiden catch at Fleetwood in April, 1908 for the Crown Steam Fishing Company. The Trawler was sold to French ownership in 1915. At the Elevator berth is the steel-hulled, 3 mast Norwegian barque *Delta*, registered at Christiania (Oslo) and which was built as the *Odd* in 1891. This photograph is thought to date from about 1910.

Merchant Schooner.

Hundreds of schooners of the type illustrated here worked round the coasts of Britain and her continental neighbours in the nineteenth century and in the first decades of the 1900s. The top-sail schooner in this photograph is typical of those schooners built in the North West and which ranged in size from 140 to 200 tons gross. Two and three masted schooners of this type were built in Fleetwood between 1860 and 1890 by the firm of John Gibson & Sons and others were built for Fleetwood owners at the shipyard in nearby Glasson Dock. Wine, oranges, slate, flax, pit-props, iron and barrelled herring were some of the the cargoes carried to Fleetwood by these fine sailing vessels.

Jersey Potatoes.

New potatoes, barrelled and stacked above and below deck on the Goole Steam Shipping Company's coaster *Ouse*, 682 gross tons, built by Dobson and Company at Newcastle in 1884. Jersey potatoes were a regular seasonal cargo to Fleetwood from 1899 onwards, the first such cargo arriving in that year brought by the steamer *Altona*, another of the Goole Steam Shipping Company's early vessels. This East-coast based shipping company always worked closely with the Lancashire & Yorkshire Railway Company, who owned and operated Fleetwood's docks, and in 1905 the L&Y Railway purchased outright the Goole Steam Shipping Company. The railway company retained the distinctive black-topped yellow funnel with its red band as the funnel livery for its east-coast fleets. The potatoes brought directly from the Channel Islands to Fleetwood by these ships were distributed to markets throughout the North West by the railway company.

James Fisher & Sons of Barrow owned the steam coaster *Stream Fisher*.

Seen here in Glasson Dock, *Stream Fisher* was typical of Fisher's vessels of the 1920s and 1930s when salt, limestone, coal and gravel were cargoes handled at Fleetwood. Ships of the Fisher's fleet came to Fleetwood from the Company's earliest years when their fleet of schooners, which by the turn of the century was the U.K.'s largest schooner fleet, often traded into and out of the port. Their last schooner was sold in 1921 but Fisher's steam coasters continued to call in Fleetwood and their funnel letter 'F' was often seen at Fleetwood's quayside.

Ship to Rail cargo working at Fleetwood's riverside quay wall.

A photograph from the early 1900s with a small steam coaster moored alongside the wall. Beyond the coaster a vessel in the Railway's fleet of Belfast packet-steamers can be seen. The railway sidings, the cluster of buildings along the railway sidings and the clutter usually found around sea-ports – note the ship's boat placed between the converging tracks – all have now gone. The site is occupied by the trailer-park for the Roll-on ferry service.

M.V. Rasmus Throlstrup.

Photographed at Fleetwood in September, 1964 bringing Vinyl Chloride from Pasedena, USA for ICI Limited. This Liquified Gas Carrier was built at Marstrand in 1953. Photo P. Horsley.

Consulting the Harbour Master, a scene captured in July, 1961 when *Herriesdale* (ex. *Cromarty Firth*) visited Fleetwood with a consignment for ICI's Hillhouse plant. The Glasgow registsred *Herriesdale* was built at Aberdeen in 1937 under the 'Scrap and Build' programme during the recession years of that era. In Greek ownership the vessel later became the *Georgios Ventouris* and, later still, *Maria Preka*, remaining in service as a Mediterranean trader well into the 1980s. Photo P. Horsley.

Vinyl Chloride being discharged from the specialist Liquified Gas carrier *Rasmus Throlstrup*. Road tankers were located in specially rigged bays to receive their loads for transit to the nearby ICI complex. Photo P. Horsley.

The loading and discharging of cargo often continued through the hours of darkness and here a Chemical Tanker is being loaded from ICI road tankers, part of the inter-plant traffic between the various sites operated by ICI Limited. The ICI Hillhouse complex, close by Wyre Dock, has always been a bulk producer of Alkali based products. Photo P. Horsley.

A sequence of photographs taken in January, 1965 as the Greek registered cargo vessel *Eleni K* docked at Fleetwood with a cargo of synthetic resin from Italy. With a marked starboard list, the 336 foot (102 metres) long vessel with a beam measurement of 14 metres was eased through the 15 metres wide lock and to her berth with the aid of the two Fleetwood tugs *Cleveleys* and *Landy*. *Eleni K* was a ship which had many names and many owners over the years and on her arrival in Fleetwood, her ownership in dispute, an Admiralty Writ was 'nailed' to her mast. Built in 1939 as *Mosdale* she became in turn *Albion Star*, *Balzac*, *Carroll*, *Norman Star* and then *Basil* before becoming *Eleni K* under the Greek flag. Photographs by P. Horsley.

The Seville registered cargo vessel *Villa Blanca*, 2334 gross tons ex. *Bretagne*, photographed in Wyre Dock in August, 1970. In 1971, Castaner y Ortiz/Golfo Lines established a twice-weekly service between Fleetwood, Bilbao and Santander bringing fruit and vegetables to Fleetwood and taking general cargo outward. The trade proved insufficient and the service ended after only a few years. Photo P. Horsley.

Wyre Dock scene in 1972.

Four merchant vessels together in the dock, evidence of Fleetwood's revived commercial traffic during the 1970s. Readily identifiable are *Uffe*, *Perleus* and *Simo*. Photo P. Horsley.

Many small coasters have used the port and have carried a variety of cargoes including paraffin wax, sulphur, drums of carbide, melons, tea, potatoes, butter, lard, onions and grapefruit. Many of these coasters left Fleetwood in ballast to collect new cargoes elsewhere but outward shipments from Fleetwood have included Soda ash, Nitro-chalk, glass from St Helens, cars and vans from Ford Motors, structural steelwork, tractors and scrap metal.

The Dutch coaster, *Schokland,* seen here in Fleetwood, was typical of the small Dutch coastal 'tramps' often called 'Groningers' after their home port. Many were owned by their Captain and often crewed by members of his family. This photograph of *Schokland* was taken in 1967 as a member of her crew was taking the opportunity to work on the partly painted hull of his ship. Photo by P. Horsley.

Arktis a German built 498 gross tons general cargo vessel photographed in 1974 bringing telegraph poles from Finland as Fleetwood's timber importing trade experienced a revival in the 1970s and 80s. Timber imports, once one of Fleetwood Dock's principal commodities, had radically declined in the twenty years between 1919 and 1939 and became relatively insignificant as the port of Preston took an increasing part of the North West's timber importing traffic. Then, in 1968, the firm of Calder & Grandidge Ltd. came to Fleetwood and established a Depot and creosoting plant on Wyre Dock specialising in the handling of telegraph poles and railway sleepers. Many shipments of timber, mainly from Baltic Ports, again came to Fleetwood but the underground cabling of the telephone system and the change to concrete sleepers by British Rail brought Fleetwood's revived timber trade to an end. Photo P. Horsley.

Ulster Merchant.

Container traffic from Fleetwood to Northern Ireland began in the 1950s with vessels of the Fisher Group from Barrow ferrying out of Fleetwood the small 'railways' type container boxes. That Fleetwood - Belfast service ended in April, 1958. Later, as containerised traffic grew, other ships were brought to Fleetwood to crane-load containers in Wyre Dock to supplement the 'Coastlink' service which operated between Heysham and Northern Ireland. Here Coastline's *Ulster Merchant,* built in Germany in 1971 as *Embdena,* is seen outward bound from Fleetwood in 1974 loaded with containers and trailers. This service was superseded in 1975 when the P&O Group inaugurated the Fleetwood-Larne RO-RO vehicle service. Photo by P. Horsley.

Fleetwood Tankers Limited

Fleetwood Tankers, a part of the Boston Group, operated a fleet of small coastal tankers consisting of six different vessels over the years which served to supply fuel oil and diesel from Heysham and Stanlow to the smaller ports of the North West. *Onward Progress*, 345 tons gross, was the largest vessel to serve in the Company's fleet bringing fuel to Fleetwood. The other vessels which were in the Fleetwood Tankers fleet over the years were *Onward Enterprise*, *Onward Mariner*, *Onward Venture* and the *Onward Pioneer,* 164 tons gross and the smallest ship in the fleet. Onward was the motto of the town of Fleetwood from 1893 to 1974, after which date the town became a part of the newly created District of Wyre Borough.

Onward Enterprise, coastal tanker built at Elmshorn in 1960 as *Mathea* and photographed at Fleetwood in 1967. After Fleetwood Tankers Ltd. ended their fuel service to Wyre Dock the vessel eventually went to Tyne-Tees Waste Disposals Limited. Photo. P. Horsley.

Onward Venture, built in 1962 and photographed off Fleetwood in 1967. Photo. P.Horsley.

Onward Mariner built at the Knottingley yard of J. Harker Ltd. in 1971 and photographed in 1974. In 1985 the vessel was transferred to Allantone Supplies Ltd. of Felixtowe and in 1990 to Britannia Marine of Lowestoft,but remained Fleetwood registered. Photo. P.Horsley.

Fleetwood Salt Works

I.C.I.'s private jetty at Burn Naze on the banks of the River Wyre.

Taken after the completion of the Southern arm of the jetty in 1924, two old coasters can be seen at the jetty, neither of which appear to be the Company's own vessels judging by the funnel markings. Photo. courtesy of I.C.I. Limited.

Extensive deposits of high grade rock salt at Preesall, across the river from Fleetwood, were discovered in 1872 and by 1885 a shaft of some 186 metres deep had been sunk. Salt was pumped to the surface as brine and piped across the river Wyre to the Fleetwood Salt Works, opened at Burn Naze in 1889, where extremely pure white salt was evaporated from the brine. In 1890, the Fleetwood Salt Works were acquired by the United Alkali Company who extended the works and who also converted much of the salt extraction at Preesall to rock-salt mining. More shafts were sunk one, at least, to a depth of 360 metres and a jetty was built at Preesall in 1893 from which rock-salt was shipped. At Burn Naze, on the Fleetwood side of the river, the Northern arm of a private jetty was completed in February 1893. Soda Ash (Sodium Carbonate) was then shipped out from Burn Naze in some of the vessels which, in an almost continuous shuttle service, brought limestone from Raynes quarries in North Wales, a basic chemical for the conversion process at the Alkali Works.

The United Alkali Company's coasters, and sometimes others engaged from Savage's Zillah Shipping and Carrying Company or from W.S.Kennaugh and Company, collected limestone at Llanddulas pier and could complete the round trip from Burn Naze to North Wales and back in 24 hours. Company vessels completing 28 trips per month earned a £5 bonus for the members of the crew. As was customary in coastal vessels, the members of the crew supplied and cooked their own food and provided their own bedding. Men in the Company's ships seeking bonus rates certainly saw very little of their families at their homes in Fleetwood or Burn Naze or Thornton, even though their 'home base' was almost in sight of their houses.

The Burn Naze jetty was extended in 1924 by the completion of a Southern arm. There was no water at either the Burn Naze or the Preesall jetties at low tide and both sites were subject to heavy silting. Soda Ash and other products from the Works were shipped to Glasgow, Dublin and Belfast and to Liverpool for re-export. The United Alkali Company became a part of Imperial Chemical Industries in 1926. Mining at Preesall ended in 1930 and the Preesall jetty was demolished in 1934, salt extraction then being confined to brining. The Burn Naze jetty was last used in 1964 and demolished shortly afterwards.

S.S. Prestonian high and dry at Preesall pier.

The 223 ft. *Prestonian* was built by the Ailsa Shipbuilding Company at Troon in 1901 for a consortium of Preston businessmen. Preston Dock opened in 1892 and was attracting an expanding trade, the local leaders formed their company "Steamship Prestonian Limited" to operate their own ship from the town's new dock. *Prestonian* is seen here loading rock salt at the Preesall jetty. Later, in Liverpool ownership, the ship was generally engaged in shipping wood-pulp from Scandinavian ports to Preston and Liverpool. Photo. courtesy of Mr. Ian Baxter.

Hermann loading rock-salt at the Preesall jetty.

The 214 g.tons Flensberg registered German steam coaster *Hermann*, built at Rostock in 1890 and seen here at the Preesall jetty in 1906. This little coaster was comfortably afloat at High-tide where only vessels drawing less than 2.75 metres could load with safety. Photo. courtesy of Mr. Ian Baxter.

S.S.Sodium.

Sodium, 608 gross tons, was the last coal-fired steam coaster working to the I.C.I.'s Burn Naze jetty. Built for the United Alkali Company in 1923 by Rennoldson's at South Shields, the vessel is shown here in her original United Alkali livery. The machinery-aft steamer worked with an eight man crew - Master, Mate, Chief and 2nd. engineers, two firemen and two seamen. Other steam coasters in the Company fleet which served Fleetwood were *Helium* and the *Lithium*, both built in 1917, *Calcium* built in 1918 and *Barium*, also built in 1918 and one of the earliest British merchant vessels to have a 'Goal-post' mast. Photo. courtesy of I.C.I. Limited.

S.S. Sodium at Burn Naze.

Sodium is seen in this photograph in her later I.C.I. livery which was grey hull and a blue funnel with the I.C.I. logo. Here the vessel is loading Soda Ash which was regularly shipped to Glasgow, Belfast, Dublin, or to Liverpool. Masters of these vessels had to make at least six trips per year navigating into the Mersey to retain the Licence enabling them to sail to Mersey ports without engaging a pilot. *Sodium* worked to Burn Naze until 1964. Photo, courtesy of I.C.I. Limited.

M.V.Calcium.

The motor coaster *Calcium*, 643 gross tons, was built at Goole in 1959. She took the name of the earlier coal-fired steamer built in 1918 and mined in Liverpool Bay during the Second World War. In this photograph the ship is seen when Limestone from North Wales is being unloaded by grab-crane to waggons on the Company's internal rail system at Burn Naze. *Calcium* was sold to the Shamrock Shipping Co. Ltd. in 1967 as *Clonlee*. Photo. courtesy of I.C.I. Limitied.

M.V. Thorium, 604 gross tons, built 1947.

Another vessel in the I.C.I. fleet of Liverpool registered coasters which spent much of their time carrying 600 ton cargoes of Limestone from Llanddulas to Burn Naze. On 11th January, 1951 *Thorium*, sailing from North Wales to the Wyre with her hold full of stone, began to take in water as she neared the Wyre Light. The ship was beached well clear of the Wyre Channel and with all the hull submerged her six man crew were rescued by the Fleetwood Lifeboat *Ann Letitia Russell*. After the rescue the *Thorium* later drifted across the buoyed channel and capsised on Barnett Sands just clear of the navigable channel. The ship was eventually salvaged, being finally brought into port to complete her journey when she entered Fleetwood on 1st June, 1951 in the hands of a salvage team of the Liverpool and Glasgow Salvage Association. Photo. courtesy of I.C.I. Limited.

I.C.I. coasters strike-bound at Fleetwood during the course of a Seamens' strike and moored together at Fleetwood's old North End staging. The four ships are *Cerium*, *Thorium*, *Sodium* and the little 132 foot *M.V. Polythene*. Photo. courtesy of I.C.I. Limited.

Freight Vehicle Ferry Services to Ireland

In 1973 work began at Fleetwood to build a Roll-on/Roll-off heavy duty Link-span berth at the site of Fleetwood's original riverside quays. The venture was initiated by the then port owners, the British Transport Docks Board, in association with the P&0 group who contracted to operate through their subsidiary, Pandoro Ferries Limited, a freight service to Northern Ireland. The Ro-Ro berth has a quay length of 150 metres and can accommodate vessels of up to 152 metres length, 20.3 metres beam and 4.2 metres draught. The link-span jetty can take loads up to 180 tonnes and with two-lane working regularly turns round fully laden ferries within four hours.

The Pandoro service to Larne began in 1975 with *Bison*, *Buffalo* and, later, *Jaguar* working the regular sailings. B&I Lines Ltd. then joined with Pandoro to extend the available services to include Dublin and for some years the two companies operated a joint service with B&I's *Tipperary* augmenting the Pandoro ferries. When B&I reduced their routes, the Fleetwood-Dublin service was discontinued. Pandoro filled the vacant "slot" at the Ro-Ro berth by co-operating with Merchant Ferries Ltd. who operated a service from Fleetwood to Warren Point to augment their Heysham-Warren Point route. Pandoro, and companies with which they have co-operated over the years, have brought various vessels to Fleetwood and, in addition to the ships already listed above, have brought to Fleetwood *Scandinavia*, *Cerdic Ferry*, *Stena Trailer*, *Union Melbourne*, *Ibex*, *Skarvoy*, *Viking Trader*, *Puma* (ex. *Union Melbourne*) *Merchant Victor* and the *Merchant Venture*. Most recently, at the end of 1994, the Isle of Man Steam Packet Company's *Peveril* and the former Merchant Ferries' *Merchant Valiant* have been seen at the Fleetwood Ro-Ro berth. The *Peveril* brought cars from the Isle of Man and *Merchant Valiant*, which became part of the Pandoro fleet, served to supplement the company's regular ships on the Fleetwood-Larne service.

Pandoro Ferries' stern-loading vehicle ferry *Bison*.

The *Bison*, seen here working the Fleetwood - Larne service in 1977 joined with her sister-ship *Buffalo* to operate the route in the first years of the service. Built by J.J. Sietas at Hamburg in 1974 the vessel was powered by Klockner-Humbolt diesels and powerful side thrusters enabled her to rotate comfortably in the River Wyre alongside the Link-span berth. After having been transferred to work on other routes for some years, *Bison* was re-fitted in 1995 and enlarged with an additional deck built up at the stern and has returned to work in the Fleetwood service. Photo. P. Horsley.

The freight-vehicle ferry *Buffalo* approaching Morecambe Bay.

An aerial view taken in 1981 and giving a totally different aspect from that seen at Fleetwood by people watching from the ferry beach. There, at sea level, watchers look upwards as these high-sided ships pass by only a few metres from the water's edge. Photo. P. Horsley.

Fleetwood's Link-span ferry berth viewed from the Fleetwood Museum which is housed in the port's original Custom House on Queen's Terrace. B&I Line's *Tipperary*, built in Japan in 1979, is at 6310 tons gross and 150 metres long one of the largest vessels to have worked from the port. The B&I Line shared the use of the Fleetwood berth with Pandoro Limited for some years and a joint service to Dublin was offered along with Pandoro's Northern Ireland service. *Tipperary* has now become *Norcape* in the North Sea Ferries Group. Photo. P. Horsley.

Merchant Victor.

The vehicle ferry *Merchant Victor* of Merchant Ferries Limited casting off from Fleetwood's Ro-Ro berth. Built at Bremmerhaven, Germany, in 1978 the 1598 gross tons vessel was added to the Merchant Ferries' fleet in 1990. The Company was formed in 1986 and started a Heysham - Warren Point service which was augmented in 1989 when the "Mid-night" slot at the Fleetwood berth was utilised by the Company. Merchant Ferries Ltd. ended their link with Fleetwood in September, 1993. Presently the company provides a Heysham - Dublin service and has become a part of the Mersey Docks and Harbour Board Group. Photo. P. Horsley.

Viking Trader in the Wyre Channel.

Viking Trader ex. *Stena Trader*, built at Rendsburg in 1977 and considerably updated since joining Pandoro's fleet, is presently one of the ships regularly employed on the six days a week service to Ireland. In earlier years the ship has been owned or chartered by several groups and has sailed successively as *Goya*, *Federal Nova*, *Caribbean Sky*, *Manure VII*, and *Oyster Bay*. In 1996 the vessel has again acquired a new name and now sails as *Leopard*.

Chapter 2

Fishing Vessels :
Sail, Steam & Motor Trawlers

For many years Fleetwood was perhaps best known to most people for its large fishing fleet. Fleetwood was the third largest trawler port in the UK and the largest West coast fishing port.

Before the town and port of Fleetwood was created in the 1830s on what were then the barren dunes and warrens of the Hesketh-Fleetwood family's estates, fishermen from Knott End and Hambleton on the East bank of the Wyre fished in Morecambe Bay and the inshore waters of the Irish Sea. As the town of Fleetwood grew, and in the years between 1830 and 1890 the population grew from a couple of families in their cottages to a township of almost 10,000 persons, it presented a market for fresh fish which the district's original fishermen could not satisfy. Fishing vessels, and later the fishermens' families, came to Fleetwood from other Lancashire fishing villages and from Scotland, Brixham and the East Coast fishing ports. By 1890 Fleetwood's well established fishing fleet consisted of 35 small 'prawners' and 60 deep-sea sailing smacks. The Lancashire & Yorkshire Railway and the London & North Western Railway jointly offered a ready service to the inland markets and had provided accommodation and facilities for the fish trades.

In 1891 steam trawlers began to work from the port and the fleet quickly expanded. Within a few years 80 steam trawlers were based at the port and trawlers from other ports regularly landed their catches at Fleetwood when the West coast grounds were being exploited. Fleetwood became the country's principal port for Hake, a variety of fish then much in demand by the catering trades. As the years passed, particularly in the period after 1945 when many large trawlers began to be brought into the port, the Icelandic fishing grounds provided the greater part of Fleetwood's fish landings. Modern trawlers became very efficient, steam was replaced by diesel, and in 1966 the port's

first stern-fishing freezer trawler joined the fleet. When the Icelandic "Cod Wars" were resolved in Iceland's favour, Fleetwood's fishing industry experienced a rapid decline. Today, no large deep-sea trawlers work from the port and Fleetwood's fleet is made up of small inshore vessels and Home-water trawlers of less than 30 metres length. Landings to the fish-market are augmented by fish brought overland from Scotland and from other British ports.

In 1995, Fleetwood's fishing heritage has been marked by the return to the port of the 615 ton stern trawler *Jacinta*, one of Fleetwood's large trawlers built in 1972. The ship has been given to local enthusiasts by J. Marr & Son whose link with Fleetwood dates back to 1898. A local group, the '*Jacinta Charitable Trust*' has been formed to restore, preserve and exhibit the vessel in the Fleetwood Marina to recall the story of the Fleetwood fishing fleets and of the fishermen who manned them.

Fleetwood's fleet of sailing smacks in 1890.

A sailing "Nobby".

Locally referred to as a 'Morcambe Bay Prawner' the nobby, a single mast half-deck fishing vessel,was the type of small fishing boat common to most of the fishing ports and harbours of the North West coast of England in Victorian and Edwardian days. Gaff rigged and with a long running bowsprit, this design presented a remarkably large sail area in relation to the size of the hull and yet was readily handled by her two-man crew. One particular feature was the long, overhanging, elliptical counter stern.

Milo FD19.

A dandy rigged two-masted deep-sea sailing trawler typical of the fishing vessels which created Fleetwood's fishing industry in the years before the advent of steam trawlers. Many of these smacks were built in Fleetwood and others at nearby Glasson Dock, but many others came to Fleetwood from other fishing centres. *Milo* was built by the Hoad Brothers in Rye, Sussex, in 1865, operated from Grimsby from 1877 to 1888 and then in that year was brought to Fleetwood when she was purchased by George Miller, a local butcher who also owned several fishing smacks. *Milo* was broken up in 1916.

Steam Trawler *Gothic*.

The first steam trawler ordered and built new for Fleetwood's fishing fleet, *Gothic* was launched in 1895 from the North Shields yard of Edwards Bros. Limited. It is interesting to note that when new, as shown in this photograph, the trawler was fitted to use a beam trawl of the type also employed by the sailing trawlers. The Otter-board trawl-door nets superseded the beam trawl on the steam trawlers very shortly after the *Gothic* had joined the fishing fleet. The iron hulled *Gothic* was owned by John Kelsall and managed by Kelsall Bros. & Beeching. Transferred to Hull in 1899 the ship was lost, 'Overwhelmed in high seas', in January 1910.

Steam Trawler *Oceanic*. Built in 1896.

This 168 ton trawler was built at Grimsby by Thomas Charlton and registered there as a new vessel in March, 1896. The trawler had been built for Mr. Robert Kelsall and almost immediately was sent to work with the Kelsall Bros. & Beeching's 'Gamecock' fleet which at the time was working out of Fleetwood. In August, 1897 the ship's registry was transferred to Fleetwood and the trawler took the Fleetwood Fishing No. FD187. This photograph, from an original glass plate negative in the Peter Horsley Collection, was taken after the vessel had been transferred to Hull and is believed to date from about 1902.

Swift FD 170 Steam Trawler and Fish Carrier.

Built at Howden-on-Tyne in 1897, *Swift* was registered at Fleetwood as a new vessel on 9th June, 1897 and operated as the fish carrier for the 'Boxing' fleet of her owners Messrs. Kelsall Bros & Beeching. Larger and faster than the other ships in the fleet which, having set their catch in boxes, would transfer the catch using the ships' boats to ferry the boxes to *Swift* for quick delivery to port for marketing whilst the remainder of the fleet continued at the fishing.

Gothic, Martin, Plover, Wren, Quail, Hawk, Gull, Jay and *Dove* were all steam trawlers built for the 'Boxing' fleet of Kelsall & Beeching during the years when it operated out of Fleetwood. Kelsall and Beechings's fleet transferred to Hull in 1898/1899 and *Swift* then fished out of Hull until being scrapped in 1936.

Fleetwood's riverside quay crowded with sailing smacks and early steam trawlers at the turn of the Century.

The riverside quay is tidal and vessels ground at low water. The larger steam trawlers in the fleet began to make use of the enclosed Wyre Dock, earlier used exclusively for cargo traffic, from 1902 onwards and a temporary fish market was established in former Goods-sheds there. The building of Fleetwood's Fish Dock began in 1908.

FD208 Margaret making out of Fleetwood.

Margaret, a 64ft (19.5m) 51 tons ketch-rigged smack, was built for R&W Leadbetter in 1903, some twelve years after steam trawlers had begun to work from the port. One of the last sailing smacks to join Fleetwood's fishing fleet, *Margaret* was the first of the Fleetwood smacks to be motorised, an auxiliary petrol engine was fitted in 1923. The vessel remained in the ownership of the Leadbetter family, but with a few shares held by the Coulburn Brothers of Freckleton, rope makers, and by Thomas Rigby of Fleetwood, sailmaker, until 1939 when the managing ownership passed to Mr J. Wignall. Although remaining Fleetwood registered, the smack later worked out of nearby Glasson Dock until she was acquired by J.R. Sheeder of Hartlepool.

The old fashioned, iron headed wooden beam trawl, clearly seen lying over the stern, continued in use in the sailing smacks long after steam trawlers brought Otterboard trawls into use.

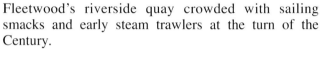

34

FD208 Margaret entering Ramsey, Isle of Man, under full sail.

Akranes FD 33 taking on ice from the old Ice-House.

A photograph of trawlers in Fleetwood Dock shortly before 1914. The steam trawler *Akranes* in the forefront of the picture was built by Edwards Bros. in North Shields in 1898. One of the early trawlers in the fleet of J. Marr & Son, the vessel was brought to Fleetwood in February, 1905. A relatively small ship at 114ft (34.7m) and 185 gross tons, nevertheless, the little wheelhouse-abaft trawler sometimes fished the Icelandic grounds. The trawler *Evelyn FD59*, built in 1906, lies astern of the *Akranes* and beyond her is the *Scomber FD90* of 1909. Almost abreast of *Akranes* is *FD77 Merrydale*. Transferred to Grimsby owners in 1918, *Akranes* was later sold into Dutch registry as *Anna Josina*.

Fleetwood Fish Market in the late 1920s.

Merisia FD153.

The design and fitting of steam trawlers made rapid strides in the first decades of the 20th Century. Trawlers became much larger, they had powerful and more efficient engines, larger fish-rooms were possible and powerful larger capacity winches were installed. Flush decks were replaced by raised forecastles and the wheelhouse was enclosed. *Merisia*, built at Selby in 1912, had all these improvements. A very successful trawler in Fleetwood's trawler fleets, owned first by the Fleetwood Steam Trawler Company and later by the Alberic Steam Fishing Company, *Merisia* was lost in Laxey Bay, Isle of Man, with all her 12 man crew in January, 1940.

Phyllis Rosalie, in 1934 Fleetwood's newest trawler.

The Boston Deep Sea Fishing Company took delivery of *Phyllis Rosalie* in 1934 and in 1935, with her Skipper Walter 'Fly' Holmes, the ship represented the Port's fishing industry at King George V's Silver Jubilee Spithead Review. Here, a dense pall of black smoke demonstrating her coal fired steam plant, the vessel is seen steaming out of the Wyre Dock lock. Later in 1935 the trawler was taken up by the Admiralty and became the Anti-Submarine trawler *HMT Amethyst*, lost on active service in December 1940, when she was mined in the Thames Estuary.

What fishing is all about.

A fine haul of Hake, Fleetwood's premier fis[h]
photographed as the net was hauled aboard the Fleetwo[od]
Steam Trawler *Robert Murray* in 1937. Photo courtesy
John Noble.

Trawlers preparing for sea at Fleetwood's North-end staging.

The lock giving access to Wyre Dock was not deep enough to permit large, deep-draught trawlers to pass out of the dock fully laden with fuel, ice, water and stores. The lock sill was lowered in 1952 but prior to that date the port's larger trawlers left the dock only partly readied for sea and topped up ice, water and stores and took on the full crew at the North-end staging. In this photograph *Westella FD318* and *Andradite H26* are nearest the camera. Built at Beverley as *Dervish* for Hellyer Bros. of Hull and in Admiralty service during the war years as *HMT. Pearl*, the 426 gross tons trawler *Westella* was brought to Fleetwood in 1946 by J. Marr and Son Ltd. *Andradite*, too, was originally a Hull ship and in the fleet of the Kingston Steam Fishing Company. After war service as a minesweeper she was brought to Fleetwood in 1949 by J. Marr and Son and worked out of the port until, after stranding in 1957, she was scrapped in 1959.

Red Hackle.

A fine view of the oil-fired steam trawler *Red Hackle* making her way into the Fish dock. Built by John Lewis & Son at Aberdeen in 1950, the trawler was owned by Captain E.D.W. Lawford's Iago Steam Trawling Company. All the Iago ships were registered at London and bore London Fishing-numbers. *Red Hackle* was originally registered as L0109 but in 1953 was chosen to be one of two Fleetwood trawlers to represent the port's fleet at the Coronation Spithead Review. *Red Hackle* was re-registered at Fleetwood and given the fishing-number FD304, the only Iago trawler to have a Fleetwood registration. The other Fleetwood trawler at that Review was the Boston Deep Sea Fisheries' *Princess Royal*. In 1954 *Red Hackle* was sold to Hull's Lord Line and there renamed *Lord Hawke*.This ship was scrapped in 1968.

The trawlers *Jacinta*, *Ssafa*, *Aberdeen Explorer*, *Lord Nuffield* and *Navena* landing their catches at Fleetwood's Fish Dock. Photo. P. Horsley.

Fleetwood's "Lumpers' landing a catch to the Fish-market in 1963. Photo P. Horsley.

Caught by an ebbing tide.

The trawler *Wyre Revenge* aground at the edge of the Wyre channel in 1959. This photograph shows the lines and proportions of the sturdy deep-sea trawler as the ship is exposed awaiting the returning tide to lift her free. At Fleetwood there can be over 11m difference between High and Low water levels on some tides. Photo by P. Horsley

Motor Trawler *Josena*.

Diesel engined vessels replaced steam in the trawler fleets during the 1950s and 1960s, the port's last Steam Trawler *Samuel Hewett* being scrapped in 1968 after only twelve years service. *Josena*, typical of the diesel trawlers added to the fleets at that time, was built at Beverley in 1957 and fished from Fleetwood until being sold into foreign ownership in 1984 as Fleetwood's fleets were dispersed when the Icelandic fishing grounds closed to British trawlers. Photo P. Horsley.

Criscilla, built in the yards of Hall, Russell & Co., Aberdeen, in 1966.

The stern fishing trawler *Criscilla* of J. Marr & Son Ltd was, at 952 gross tons and 185 feet (57 metres) in length, Fleetwood's largest ever trawler. The vessel was equipped to process the catch and then to fast-freeze it into blocks of approx. 45kg for storage. *Criscilla* was the only freezer trawler to work in Fleetwood's fleet. Some of the smaller stern trawlers which worked from the port later had refrigerated fish-rooms but none had full freezer capacity. Photo P. Horsley.

Landing *Criscilla's* catch.

Palleted frozen blocks being lifted from the ship's fish-room whilst new trawl warps are prepared for the trawler's winches. The work of unloading the catch and the work needed to prepare the vessel to return to the fishing were carried out simultaneously. Photo P. Horsley.

Irvana, Maiden voyage, July 1972.

Built at Grangemouth, *Irvana* was one of several stern trawlers operating out of Fleetwood in the last years of the port's role as a major deep sea fishing port. *Irvana* was owned by J. Marr & Son, then the port's principal trawler owners who had begun their association with Fleetwood in 1898. Photo P. Horsley.

Philomena.

Typical of the small fishing vessels which now work out of Fleetwood, this Dutch built beam trawler, built at Den Helder in 1973, was photographed setting out for the Irish Sea grounds in 1992. Photo Alan Taylor.

Part of Fleetwood's Jubilee Quay, dating originally from the late 1800s, still provides the harbour and berthing for the Port's fleet of small fishing vessels. Many boats, Fleetwood owned and operated, still carry the Fishing Number and Registration of other West coast ports – Lancaster, Milford Haven and Workington registrations are prominent in this photograph.

The scene during the Fishing Strike with many ships tied up in dock. Two views giving some measure of Fleetwood's fishing fleet before the 'Cod Wars' led to the departure of the larger trawlers. Photos. P. Horsley.

Chapter 3

The Belfast Steamer Services: 1843 - 1928

For many years Fleetwood was the base for one of the principal steamer links between England and Ireland. Established as a regular service in 1843 with twice-weekly sailings between Fleetwood and Belfast, the route had been tested earlier by Fleetwood's 'founding-father' Sir Peter Hesketh - Fleetwood who, in 1841, had been able to report to the Directors of the Preston & Wyre Railway, Harbour and Dock Company that "Steamship services to Ardrossan, Londonderry, Belfast and Dublin had been established" . The Irish crossings by Sir Peter's small paddle steamers, though widely advertised, hardly constituted an established service, they were offered on an occasional basis and in reality served only to prove that a demand existed for a Fleetwood - Belfast service. In 1843 Sir Peter's former agent, Frederick Kemp, formed the North Lancashire Steam Navigation Company and regular, time-tabled passenger-cargo sailing began. At first steamers left from Fleetwood on Wedesdays and Saturdays with return sailings from Belfast on Mondays and Fridays. The number of sailings increased when the ' Joint Railways' (the Lancashire & Yorkshire and the London & North Western railway companies who owned the Preston & Wyre Railway and who had been shareholders in the North Lancs. Steam Nav. Company from its inception) took a majority shareholding in the shipping company and arranged the financing for newer, larger, vessels. By 1853 sailings each way between Fleetwood and Belfast were operated each weekday, boat-trains provided an express railway link with the service and in 1874 the joint Railways became sole owners of the steamer operation. By 1892 the service was set to a "fixed" sailing time to coincide with the train service. The London boat - train left London Euston at 5.30pm. and arrived at Fleetwood at 10.25pm. and the train from Leeds and Manchester arrived at 10.35pm., the steamer being due to sail at 10.45pm. The incoming steamer from Belfast arrived at Fleetwood at 5.45am. with trains departing for London, Manchester and Leeds shortly afterwards.

From the commencement of the service, cargo was always carried by the steamers and all the ships which served on the route were designed to carry considerable amounts of cargo as well as passengers. A large goods shed and warehouse facilities existed alongside the steamer berths at Fleetwood and as traffic increased over the years these facilities were extended. The route was also a designated Royal Mail service. The Irish cattle trade provided the most regular commercial consignments carried by the steamers and from the earliest years of the service special lower-hold provision was made for the conveyance of livestock. Similarly, special provision was made at Fleetwood to hold the cattle and other live stock, pens being constructed beneath the wooden staging of the berths and in the underground levels of the railway station buildings.These livestock facilities were also used for cattle brought from Londonderry, a route operated by various companies over the years but lastly by the 'Joint Railways' who used their older vessels for the service. The Londonderry service was abandoned in 1912 but cattle coutinued to be carried by the Belfast steamers until the last days of that service. In 1923 the London, Midland and Scottish Railway Company began to operate, taking over the services and routes previously established by the Lancashire & Yorkshire Railways, the London & North Western Railway and the Midland Railway, amongst others. Throughout the region there was duplication of services established earlier by what had been separate competing companies and it was necessary for the newly amalgamated L.M.S. to rationalise the system. In 1926 it was decided that Fleetwood was to lose the Belfast steamers, the Ulster service was to be concentrated on the former Midland Railway's more recently built harbour at Heysham and the number of ships based at Fleetwood was to be reduced. The last sailing on the Fleetwood - Belfast route, a service which had operated for 85 years, was made on Saturday, 28th April, 1928 when, at midnight, the *Duke of Cumberland* left Fleetwood's North-end steamer berth. It was the end of an era in the history of Fleetwood.

Fleet List, Fleetwood – Belfast Service 1840 - 1928

Served	Vessel	Type	Built	Notes
1840-1843	*James Dennistoun*	P.S.	Glasgow 1835	Occasional sailings for P. Hesketh-Fleetwood. Sold to Birkenhead & Chester Railway Company in 1847.
1840-1842	*Express*	P.S.	Glasgow 1836	Occasional sailings for P. Hesketh Fleetwood. Ownership transferred to the Preston & Wyre Railway in 1843.
1843-1860	*Prince of Wales*	P.S.	Glasgow 1842	Withdrawn from service, 1860.
1843-1849	*Her Majesty*	P.S.	Glasgow 1843	Wrecked off the Antrim coast in 1849.
1843-1860	*Princess Alice*	P.S.	Glasgow 1843	Served Glasgow-Londonderry 1851/2 Scrapped 1883.
1844-1851	*Royal Consort*	P.S.	Glasgow 1844	Withdrawn from service 1860.
1856-1871	*Prince Patrick*	P.S.	Liverpool 1856	Withdrawn from the route in 1871.
1861-1866	*Prince Alfred*	P.S.	Glasgow 1861	To Douglas route in 1866. Wrecked I.O.M. 1869.
1867-1877	*Prince Arthur*	P.S.	Greenock 1863	ex. *Alfred* ex. *Old Dominion*. Sold in 1877.
1870-1896	*Princess of Wales*	P.S.	Hebburn 1870	Sailed Fleetwood - Belfast for 26 years.
1873-1888	*Thomas Dugdale*	P.S.	Hebburn 1873	Sold 1888. Renamed *Laurel* (Laird's) Scrapped 1893.
1875-1893	*Duke of Connaught*	P.S.	Barrow 1875	Withdrawn 1893. Sold 1894. Scrapped 1895.
1878-1894	*Earl of Ulster*	P.S.	Barrow 1878	Sold to Harland & Wolf as accommodation ship.
1886-1896	*Prince of Wales* (2)	P.S.	Barrow 1886	Withdrawn 1895. Sold to Spanish Government 1896.
1892-1906	*Duke of Clarence*	TSS.	Birkenhead 1892	To Hull-Zeebrugge route in 1906 and scrapped in 1930.
1894-1911	*Duke of York*	TSS.	Dumbarton 1894	To IoM.S.P.Co. as *Peel Castle* in 1912.
1895-1911	*Duke of Lancaster*	TSS.	Barrow 1895	To I.o.M.S.P.Co. as *The Ramsey in 1912. Lost Aug. 1915.*
1898-1928	*Duke of Cornwall*	TSS.	Barrow 1898	To I.o.M.S.P.Co. as *Rushen Castle* in 1928.
1902-1928	*Duke of Connaught* (2)	TSS.	Clydebank 1902	To Heysham-I.o.M. route 1928. To Goole in 1930.
1907-1914	*Duke of Albany*	TSS.	Clydebank 1907	To Admiralty service 1914. Sunk by U-boat in 1916.
1909-1927	*Duke of Argyll*	TrSS.	Dumbarton 1909	To Tilbury-Dunkirk service as *Alsacian* in 1927.
1909-1928	*Duke of Cumberland*	TrSS.	Dumbarton 1909	To Tilbury-Dunkirk service as *Piccard* in 1928.

Abbreviations :

P.S.   –   Paddle Steamer
TSS.   –   Twin Screw Steamer
TrSS.   –   Triple Screw Steamer

An advertisement for the Belfast steamer service which was printed in the Fleetwood Chronicle & Monthly Advertiser on Saturday, November 11th. 1843.

ORIGINAL TYPE, FLEETWOOD & BELFAST STEAMER, 1843. "HER MAJESTY". Length 160 ft., Breadth 25 ft., Depth of Hold 13 ft. 5", Registered Tonnage 312, Gross 499, Two Steeple Engines 125 H.P. each, Speed 8 Knots.

Paddle Steamer *Her Majesty*.

An advertising block print used by Frederick Kemp's North Lancashire Steam Navigation Company for the Belfast steamer service in 1846. Built by Messrs. Tod & MacGregor, Glasgow, in 1843, the ship was lost off Rathlin Island, North Antrim, in 1849 when on service to Londonderry.

P.S. *Royal Consort* from a painting in Fleetwood Museum.

Royal Consort, acquired by Frederick Kemp in 1847, was first registered at Preston but in March, 1850 the registration was transferred to Fleetwood. The 1850 entry describes the ship as iron plate on iron frame, Lengh 178ft. (54m) deck and quaterdeck, three masts schooner rigged. The vessel underwent several alterations over the years, her final configuration being shown as length 215ft. (66m) 796 gross tons and reduced to 2 masts. This painting must date from her later years, the ship remaining in railway company service operating various West coast routes until 1883.

Paddle Steamer *Prince of Wales*.

The paddle steamer here moored well upstream from the North-end passenger-steamer berths and surrounded by the sailing smacks and prawners which normally used this section of Fleetwood's riverside quays, is the *P.S. Prince of Wales*. The ship was the last paddle steamer built for the Belfast service coming from the Barrow Shipbuilding and Engineering Company in 1886. The vessel was withdrawn from service in 1895 and lay in Fleetwood until being sold to Spain in June, 1896 for Government service.

No 4. Zeebrugge
Hull Boat "Duke of Clarence".

Duke of Clarence.

Built by Laird Bros. at Birkenhead in 1892, *Duke of Clarence* was the prototype vessel for the joint-railways' fleet of Twin-screw steamers built for the Fleetwood-Belfast sevice. *"Clarence"* was employed on the route until June, 1906 when the Lancashire & Yorkshire Railway Company took sole ownership of the vessel and transferred her to Goole, their East-coast base, to provide a summer-season passenger-cargo service between Hull and Zeebrugge in Belgium. Though registered at Goole , the ship was usually laid-up at Fleetwood during the winter months and short cruises were offered by the company as she left her East coast station to steam to Fleetwood. The Autumn cruise was South-about, Hull to Fleetwood via the Channel Islands whilst the Spring cruise was North-about, Fleetwood to Hull via the Hebrides and Northern Isles. This photograph from an old Belgian Railways postcard shows the gilded decoration on the ship's stern, a feature on all ships built for the Fleetwood-Belfast service. *Duke of Clarence* was broken-up at Barrow in 1930.

Duke of Connaught.

The second *Duke of Connaught* from an official Lancashire & Yorkshire Railway Company postcard. Built by John Brown & Company at Clydebank in 1902 for the Fleetwood-Belfast service, the ship was a fine passenger-cargo vessel of 1680 gross tons, length 315ft. (96m). Capable of a speed of 20 Knots, the ship could carry 900 passengers and was employed on the Belfast route until 1928. Owned then by the L.M.S.Railway Company the ship was transferred to Heysham to operate on the Heysham-Isle of Man service until, in 1930, being sent round to the East coast to work on the Hull-Zeebruge route. The ship was scrapped in the Netherlands in 1934.

THE "DUKE OF CONNAUGHT."
FLEETWOOD AND BELFAST SERVICE.

Fleetwood's Wyre Dock, April 1912.

The scene in Wyre Dock during a coal-miners' strike when ships all round the country were laid-up for want of fuel. In the picture three of the "Ducal fleet" of the L.& Y.R/L.N.W.R's Belfast steamers can be identified. *Cornwall*, *Connaught* and *Clarence* are the three outer vessels at the dockside.

Duke of Albany.

Built at John Brown's yard, Clydebank, in 1907 the *Duke of Albany* was the last of the single funnel twin-screw steamers built for the Fleetwood-Belfast service. Larger than the other twin-screw ships which had preceded her in the fleet, *"Albany"* had a length of 330ft.(101m) and a gross tonnage of 2259 gt. *Duke of Albany* had only a few years service as a Belfast steamer. Requisitioned by the Admiralty in 1914 the ship served in the North Sea areas as an armed boarding-vessel but was torpedoed and sunk by U.27 on August 25th . 1916.

Belfast steamers at Fleetwood's North-end passenger berths. Photo. courtesy of John Noble.

Duke of Cumberland aground in the River Wyre, March 1921.

The two-funnelled, triple-screw steamer *Duke of Cumberland* came into service in 1909 along with her sister ship *Duke of Argyll*. Both ships had direct-drive turbine engines and were built by Denny at Dumbarton. To the *Duke of Cumberland* came the sad task of operating the last sailing from Fleetwood when the route was closed in 1928, the vessel was then transferred to the Tilbury - Dunkirk route (later Folkestone - Dunkirk) and re-named *Piccard*. In 1936 the ship was sold into Greek ownership and re-named *Heliopolis*.

Fleetwood 1917, *Duke of Argyll* in Wartime livery.

During the 1914 - 1918 War the route between Fleetwood and Belfast was a major link between England and Ireland. Service personnel, stores and ammunition to Northern Ireland and men, horses and fodder to England seem to have been the principal users of the service but cargoes of cattle, bacon and butter also came to help to keep people supplied with food. The service was maintained unbroken throughout the war and the ships sailed unescorted - they relied on dazzle-paint and their superior 21 knot speed to evade enemy U-boats.

Duke of Argyll in L.M.S. livery.

A photograph taken after the formation of the London, Midland & Scottish Railway Company which took place in January 1923. In 1927 the ship was transferred to operate on the Tilbury-Dunkirk route in the fleet of the French based company - Angleterre-Lorraine-Alsace Societe Anonyme de Navigation and re-named *Alsacien*. The ship was scrapped in 1936.

Chapter 4

Links with the Isle of Man

Fleetwood's link with the Isle of Man began in the earliest years of the port's development. Sir Peter Hesketh-Fleetwood, keen to promote the trade and traffic to his newly built town and harbour, employed the 104 ft. Paddle Steamer *James Dennistoun* to pioneer services to Douglas. An advert dated July 3rd.1840 read :- ***For the Isle of Man. Pleasure trip to Douglas, Isle of Man. The fine steamer James Dennistoun will leave Fleetwood for Douglas for a pleasure excursion on Saturday August 15th. 1840 at 10 o'clock in the morning returning on the Monday following. Passage there and back six shillings. Refreshments provided on board on moderate terms. James Dennistoun, steamer. Charles Edwards, Master. A band will be in attendance***.

The railway connecting Fleetwood with inland Lancashire had opened one month earlier and it was hoped that regular services to ports round the Irish Sea would develop. However, only the Belfast service prospered and, indeed, continued for 85 years. The Isle of Man link failed to develop into an all-year-round service despite several attemps to establish such a route. Frederick Kemp's North Lancashire Steam Navigation Company introduced an all-year-round twice-weekly service from Fleetwood to the Island in 1845 first using his paddle steamer *Orion* (Built 1841) and then *Fenella* (Built 1846). This service was abandoned in December, 1846 and Fleetwood's link with the Isle of Man reverted to the seasonal summer service begun by the Isle of Man Steam Packet Company's *Mona's Isle* in 1842. *Mona's Isle* was a 200 tons paddle steamer capable of a speed of 7 knots. The fare from Fleetwood to Douglas was six shillings and sixpence saloon and four shillings (20p) steerage.

Summer-season sailings between Fleetwood and Douglas were available each year between 1842 and 1876 with ships from both the I.O.M. Steam Packet Co. and the North Lancs St.Nav.Co operating the route, sometimes independently and for several years jointly, with sailing tickets interchangable between the two companies, their ships sailing on alternate days. From 1876 until 1961 ships of the I.O.M.S.P.Co. alone served the route on a daily basis between June and September each year.

Over those years most of the Steam Packet Company's ships have at one time or another served on the Fleetwood route. The ships regularly in service to Fleetwood have been *Mona's Queen* (2) built in 1885 and on the route until 1904. *Viking* succeeded her in 1905 until 1930 when *Lady of Mann* became the principal ship to operate the Fleetwood service, though *Viking* continued to operate on the Fleetwood route at intervals right up to her withdrawal from service in 1954 and her eventual scrapping. From December, 1940 until April, 1946 the all-year-round daily service between the Island and the mainland operated between Douglas and Fleetwood. Wartime conditions dictated the transfer of the service from its normal mainland terminus of Liverpool. *Snaefell*, *Rushen Castle* (ex *Duke of Cornwall*) and *Victoria* maintained the wartime service. During the post-war years up to 1961 again most of the passenger ships in the Steam Packet Company's fleet appeared at Fleetwood at one time or another before, in 1961, Fleetwood's passenger berths were condemned as unsafe for public use and the summer-season services to the Island came to an end.

In 1968 Sir John Onslow attempted to establish a hovercraft service between Fleetwood and Douglas and formed the Norwest Hovercraft Company Limited. His small Denny hovercraft failed to achieve a service to the Isle of Man but, convinced by his market research that the route was viable, his Company chartered the 1339 gross tons Norwegian motor-vessel *Stella Marina* which successfully reopened the Fleetwood - Douglas link. The 1970 season was a failure. The former MacBraynes ship *Lochiel* (which they had renamed *Norwest Laird*) was acquired but the vessel was totally inadequate for the task - too small, too slow and too old. The service was frequently disrupted and the Hovercraft Company ceased to trade. *Lochiel* became a static restaurant and club ship at Canons March, Bristol, but was broken-up in January 1996.

In 1971 the Isle of Man Steam Packet Company prevailed upon the British Transport Docks Board to improve the dredger berth which had been built where Fleetwood's former passenger berths had stood and to convert it for use by passenger vessels. Summer-season sailings from Fleetwoood to Douglas were restored and Steam Packet Company ships were again seen at Fleetwood. Summer sailings have continued since that year but no longer on a basis of daily sailings as in the former years. More recently, *Mona's Queen* and *Lady of Mann* offered "Fun Boat" excursions to the island with onboard entertainment provided during the crossings, again a summer - season service which proved very popular. In 1994 more frequent crossings to Douglas commenced with the advent of the Company's new fast Sea-Cat craft *Seacat Isle of Man* which made her first passenger service for the Steam Packet Company when she was employed on the Fleetwood - Douglas route. Uniquely, on the 12th. July, 1994 the whole of the Steam Packet Company's then operational fleet on that one day appeared at Fleetwood - *The Seacat Isle of Man* on her scheduled excursion sailing whilst *King Orry* and the *Peveril* were diverted to Fleetwood from their normal Heysham destination due to the closure of the port of Heysham for security reasons. In 1996 Sea Containers Ltd. has become the owner of the Isle of Man Steam Packet Company and new services and routes are being introduced. 150 years after Sir Peter Hesketh - Fleetwood's exploratory services to Ireland the Company now offer Fleetwood - Dublin sailings using their popular *Lady of Mann*.

The twin-screw steam turbine ship *Manxman*.

Manxman was the last of a series of 6 Cammell Laird built steamships to join the Isle of Man Steam Packet Company's fleet designed as standard passenger ferries without drive-on facilities for cars. Often employed on the Fleetwood service, *Manxman* made her first sailing out of Fleetwood on 23rd. May 1955 and her last sailing from the port was recorded on the 15th. August,1982 just prior to her withdrawal from service and subsequent sale for static use as a restaurant and club ship. *Manxman* is the last survivor of the steam passenger-ferries. Photograph by P.Horsley.

Paddle Steamer *Mona's Queen*.

Mona's Queen (2) seen here steaming out of Fleetwood, was built by the Barrow Ship Building Company in 1885. The ship was regularly employed on the Fleetwood-Douglas service until 1904 and was the last paddle steamer to serve in the Isle of Man Steam Packet Company's fleet, not being broken-up until 1929.

Tynwald.

The twin-screw steamer *Tynwald* (3) was built at the Fairfield's yard, Govan, in 1891 and was the first ship built for the Company with a triple expansion engine and with electric lighting installed by the builders. Capable of carrying 904 passengers in First and Third class accommodation, the vessel was first employed on the Douglas - Ardrossan route but later the ship was used in the Company's general service and in the summer months was engaged in excursion sailings from Fleetwood and Blackpool. Sold by the I.O.M.S.P.Co. in 1933, the vessel was converted as a private yacht and named *Western Isles*. During the 1939 - 1945 War years the ship was in Admiralty service as HMS *Eastern Isles* and passed most of her war years as an accommodation vessel at Birkenhead.

Viking.

Built by Armstrong Whitworth Ltd. at Newcastle-on-Tyne in 1905, *Viking* was perhaps the best known of the I.O.M.S.P.Co's ships to serve on the Fleetwood - Douglas route. Driven by Parson's turbines, this direct-drive triple screw steamer was capable of 24 knots having been designed to outsail the vessels of the Midland Railway Company who operated a Heysham - Douglas steamer service. *Viking* could carry 1600 passengers and held, until the arrival of the "Sea-cat" in 1994, the record for the fastest crossing, Fleetwood - Douglas, a time of 2 hours 22 minutes achieved on 25th. May, 1907. The ship was purchased by the Admiralty in 1915 and served as the seaplane carrier HMS *Vindex*. During experimental trials, the ship is reputed to have been the first vessel from whose deck wheeled-undercarriage aeroplanes were successfully launched - the world's first aircraft carrier it could be said!

Bought back by the I.O.M.S.P.Co. in 1919 and with her old name restored, *Viking* was again employed as the principal ship on the Fleetwood - Douglas service until 1930 when the brand-new *Lady of Mann* took over the regular sailings. World War II saw *Viking* again on War-service and employed as a Troop-ship, but she returned to the Fleetwood sailings on the 18th.June,1945. *Viking* made her last service to Fleetwood on 14th.August,1954 and two days later sailed to the ship-breakers yards at Barrow.

A photograph from Edwardian days which shows quite clearly what large crowds used the Fleetwood - Douglas service and, apart from the change in dress fashions, was a sight often seen at Fleetwood typical of Saturday sailings right up to World War II.

Victoria

Built in 1907 for the South Eastern & Chatham Railway and aquired by the I.O.M.S.P. Company in 1928, *Victoria* served on most of that Company's routes until being scrapped at Barrow in 1957. The vessel was often used for the Steam Packet Company's summer services but is particularly remembered at Fleetwood as one of the ships which maintained the daily all-year-round service to the Isle of Man during World War II when Fleetwood was the mainland port for the island's link. *Victoria* also saw service as a troopship, notably at the assault landings at Arromanches on D-day, 1944.

Lady of Mann.

Watched by a crowd of sightseers on Fleetwood's Ferry Beach, *Lady of Mann* makes her first sailing out of Fleetwood, the Pride of the Isle of Man Steam Packet Company, their 'Flagship' launched to be the Company's Centenary vessel in 1930, the Company's 100th. year as a shipping company.

Lady of Mann.

From 1933 to 1939, *Lady of Mann* wore the white livery with black-topped red funnel and green boot-top at the water line which had been first used in 1932 on the *Ben-My-Chree*. *Lady of Mann* was normally on the Fleetwood service during those pre-war summer seasons and was always popular with her passengers. After distinguished war service as a Trooper, *Lady of Mann* was again one of the ships operating on the Fleetwood - Douglas route up to the late 1950's and coutinued in Company service until finally leaving Douglas on 17th.August, 1971 to go off to the scrapyard.

The 1339 gross tons M.V. *Stella Marina.*

This small but popular passenger vessel was chartered by the Norwest Hovercraft Company in 1969 to reopen the Fleetwood - Douglas service on the route which had lapsed since 1961. Built at Bremen in 1963, *Stella Marina* was Norwegian owned and registered at Fredickstad, Norway. Only 67 metres overall and unstabilised, some crossings gave passengers a hard time in adverse weather conditions but, never-the-less, the ship gave excellent service and the link between Fleetwood and the Isle of Man was restored. Photo. P. Horsley.

Manx Maid photographed at Fleetwood in 1979.

Built in 1962, this 2724 tons ship was the Isle of Man Steam Packet Company's first car ferry and also the first of the Company's vessels to be fitted with stabilisers. A very successful ship for the Company, she pioneered the Island's car ferry service and was followed in 1966 by her sister-ship *Ben-My-Chree*, the fifth of that name in the Isle of Man fleet. *Manx Maid* was the first side-loading car ferry to dock at Fleetwood. Photo.P.Horsley.

A Sealink ferry at Fleetwood.

In January,1990 the I.O.M. Steam Packet Company had Sealink's *Channel Entente* with a view to purchasing the vessel. On docking trials, the ship visited the ports normally served by the Company's vessels. Here, in her Sealink livery not previously seen at the port, *Channel Entente* was photographed sailing into Fleetwood on 13th.January,1990.Photo. P.Horsley.

King Orry.

The flagship of the Isle of Man Steam Packet Company's present fleet, *King Orry* was built at Genoa, Italy, as the train-ferry *Saint Eloi* and began service on the Dover - Dunkirk crossing in March,1975. Many modifications on the vessel were carried out during the 1980's and in 1989, after serving on various Sealink routes including several U.K. - Ireland ferry services, the ship was renamed *Channel Entente* and returned to the Dover - Calais crossing. In February,1990 the I.O.M.S.P.Co. bought the vessel and after a £3.5 million refit called their new flagship *King Orry*, the fifth of their fleet to carry that name. Photo.P.Horsley.

Chapter 5

Fleetwood Lifeboats

Fleetwood has been an active lifeboat station since March, 1859 since when 11 successive lifeboats have been on station at the port. The Fleetwood boats have been relieved as required by boats from the Royal National Lifeboat Institution's relief fleet and since 1966 inflatable inshore boats and modern 'D' class boats have also been on station at Fleetwood.

The lifeboat crews over the years have mostly come from the port's community of fishermen and boatmen and this is still largely the case today. The present sophisticated motor-lifeboat equipped with radar, navigational electronics and the latest communications equipment is far removed from the pulling and sailing boats of yesteryear but the dedication and spirit of today's lifeboatmen continue in the same traditions as the crews who have preceded them.

Relief lifeboats on station at Fleetwood over the years have been launched on 48 occasions and have been credited with saving at least 17 lives. Since the first inflatables were stationed at Fleetwood in 1966 (initially for the summer months only) these fast little craft have been called out on very many rescues and assisted numerous yachtsmen, wind surfers and incautious visitors stranded by an incoming tide. Their service has been invaluable.

Lifeboat	In Service	Times Launched	Lives Saved
An unnamed vessel	1859 – 1862	9	32
Edward Wasey	1862 – 1879	11	28
Child of Hale	1879 – 1887	15	24
Child of Hale (2)	1887 – 1892	5	13
Edith (2nd boat 1887-1892)	1892 – 1894	3	19
Maud Pickup	1894 – 1930	26	117
	1930 – 1933	*Station closed*	
Sir Fitzroy Clayton	1933 – 1935	4	4
Frederick H. Pilley	1935 – 1939	12	19
Ann Letitia Russell	1939 – 1976	205	158
Lady of Lancashire	1976 – 1989	102	99
William Street	1989 –		

Child of Hale.

Two of Fleetwood's earliest lifeboats bore the name *Child of Hale*, the first was a 34ft. (10.36m) self-righting boat which arrived in Fleetwood in September, 1879 and served until March, 1887 when another, larger, self-righting 37ft (11.3m) *Child of Hale* arrived at Fleetwood and served until 1893. Robert Wright, holder of the RNLI's Silver Medal, was Lifeboat Coxwain throughout this period. This photograph shows the second *Child of Hale* after her arrival in 1887.

Fleetwood's Lifeboatmen manning *Maud Pickup*.

Fleetwood's lifeboat for 36 years, *Maud Pickup* was a 43ft (13.1m) Watson non-self-righting sailing and pulling lifeboat built in 1894 at a cost of £875, a legacy from Mr James Pickup of Southport. David Leadbetter was Fleetwood's Coxwain at the time of one of the *Maud Pickup*'s most notable services. Called out to aid the Barque *Svalen* which was stranded on the Sunderland bank at the mouth of the River Lune. Coxwain Leadbetter then sighted the barque *Louisa* aground on Pilling Sands and as the wrecked vessel broke up was able to rescue 10 more men. Another ship, W. A. Savage's wooden-hulled twin-screw coaster *Zillah*, built at Tranmere in 1891 was then sighted aground and being overwhelmed, her crew of 5 men clinging to the masts and funnel. The lifeboat was able to manoeuvre to the side of the stricken steamer and rescue the men. In all, eighteen survivors were landed safely from the three wrecked vessels that day, June 16th 1897.

Maud Pickup under sail.

A close inshore rescue under sail was witnessed by crowds of people at Knott End and Fleetwood on 19th November, 1906. The 209 gross tons Steam Trawler *Belmont* was aground on Pilling Sands with 23 men abroad. Engineers and additional crew boarded the vessel to effect repairs, bringing to 32 the number of people on the trawler. A fierce gale blew up endangering all on board, the trawler rolling heavily and the waves washing over her. *Maud Pickup* was launched and only after several attempts in the high sea was the lifeboat able to get along side to rescue all 32 men. A great welcome was given to the returning lifeboat by the large crowd of spectators who had a grandstand view of the whole drama.

Motor Lifeboat *Sir Fitzroy Clayton*.

Fleetwood's first motor lifeboat was the *Sir Fitzroy Clayton*, a 38ft (11.6m) single petrol engined self-righting lifeboat which had earlier served at Newhaven. The boat is pictured here shortly after her arrival in 1933 being inspected by the local committee and an admiring crowd keen to see the 'new' motor lifeboat.

Wreck of the *Stella Marie*.

The 300 tons three masted auxiliary motor schooner *Stella Marie*, a fish-carrier bringing fish from the Faroe Islands, was driven ashore by mountainous seas just West of the Wyre Light off Fleetwood on 5th August 1941. These two views of the broken-backed vessel recall one of the *Ann Letitia Russell*'s most notable services. In violent seas, Coxwain Jeff Wright took the lifeboat to the schooner over which huge waves were washing and despite the danger and actual damage to the lifeboat, in which the Mechanic Syd Hill was working up to his neck in water as he tended the motors under the cowling, was able to hold position alongside the wreck long enough for the schooner's 8 man crew to leap to the lifeboat. Coxwain Wright and Mechanic Hill both gained the Royal National Lifeboat Institution's Silver Medal for their service and other members of the crew the Institution's 'Thanks on Vellum' to recognise that day's work.

RNLB *Ann Letitia Russell*.

Fleetwood's busiest lifeboat to date with 205 launches and credited with saving at least 158 lives. *Ann Letitia Russell* was based at Fleetwood until 1976. She was a 41ft. (12.5m) Watson non-self-righting twin engined lifeboat capable of a speed of 8 knots. In this photograph the boat is dressed overall and is leading the events on Fleetwood's 'Lifeboat Day'. Sold out of the Lifeboat service *Ann Letitia Russell* was converted as a yacht. Recently Fleetwood's ex-lifeboat was in Barry Dock, Glamorgan as the yacht *Angela*.

Inflatable Inshore Lifeboat.

Fleetwood's first inflatable lifeboat was boat No. 91 which was stationed at Fleetwood during the summer months of 1966 and was tractor launched from the beach after being taken to the nearest convenient launching point for any incident. Other inflatables followed on a permanent basis and in 1970 boat No. D-186 was at Fleetwood. In 1977 a hoist was placed on the then newly built liftboat-pen jetty enabling launching of the D-Class boat and a boathouse for the inflatable was provided close to the crew-room. Photo P. Horsley.

Lady of Lancashire leads in her successor *William Street*.

On the 4th October, 1989 Fleetwood's new lifeboat *William Street* arrived at the port and was led in by *Lady of Lancashire* which was then to go to take up service in the reserve fleet. When *Lady of Lancashire* had come to Fleetwood in January, 1976 her first call was to save the Fleetwood fishing vessel *Replenish* and her four man crew. The lifeboat, (No. 44-015), was a 44ft steel-hulled self-righting Waveny class boat with a top speed of 15.5 knots. A pen was built in which the then new boat was kept afloat as the old Lifeboat House was unsuited to her size and design and, no longer needed, the old wooden boathouse was demolished in 1977. After 13 years service at Fleetwood, *Lady of Lancashire's* last duty was to lead in her successor. Photograph by P. Horsley.

Chapter 6

Pleasure Steamers

A sail on the sea has been one of the attractions of a seaside holiday since the days of Queen Victoria, a "Trip round the Bay" or a steamboat cruise being within the reach of most day-trippers and holiday visitors. Fleetwood was no exception. From the earliest days of 'Fleetwood-on-Wyre', Sir Peter Hesketh-Fleetwood attracted visitors to his new town and seaside resort by offering excursion steamer trips to Glasson Dock, Bardsea (for Ulverston and the Lakes) and to Piel Island, Barrow. *Cupid*, built in Port Glasgow in 1828, *Express* built in 1836 and brought to Fleetwood in 1840, and *Nile* which operated from Fleetwood from 1843 provided these services. After 1846 the Barrow route was served by the paddle-steamer *Ayrshire Lassie* and later by *Helvellyn* which operated until 1866. Towards the end of the 1800s and into the 1900s the Railway Company tugs *Wyre*, *Lune*, *Fylde* and *Cleveleys* were often engaged for pleasure trips and for summer evening cruises. Over all these years local boatmen offered trips round the Wyre Light and sailing in Morecambe Bay. Records show local shipwrights building many 'pleasure' boats for local boatmen between 1860 and 1910.

Perhaps the most notable local pleasure steamers from the Victorian era and through into the 1930s were the ships of the Blackpool Passenger Steamboat Company. These vessels were all registered at Fleetwood and as well as Fleetwood being one of their excursion calls the ships also utilised the port for bunkering and repair and frequently used the harbour to lay up over the winter months. The first of the Blackpool ships was the 135 tons paddle steamer *Wellington* built by Wm. Allsop at Preston in 1871 and in service until 1913. The paddle steamer *Bickerstaffe* was brought into service in May 1879 and was followed in 1895 by the paddler *Queen of the North*. The other Blackpool company, the North Pier Steam Ship Company, whose ships operated from the resort, also registered at and used the facilities at Fleetwood. Their first ship was the iron framed paddle steamer *Clifton*, built at Preston in 1871 and scrapped in 1905. Their second ship was the P.S. *Belle* (ex-*Belle of Llandudno*) which worked at Blackpool from 1895 until 1923.

The Company had built the 555 gross tons paddle steamer *Greyhound* in 1895. This large paddle steamer came from the yard of Thompson & Co., Clydebank, and normally was employed on excursion sailings to Liverpool and North Wales. The vessel was sold to the Abercorn Steamship Company of Belfast in 1923 and later went to Turkish ownership. The last large steamer built for the North Pier Company was the *Deerhound*, a twin screw steam ship built by J. Jones & Son at Tranmere in 1901 but sold to the West Cornwall Steamship Company in June, 1905 for their Scilly Islands service.

An extract of the Blackpool steamer sailings advertised during September 1905 reads.......

From Central Pier:-
Queen of the North to Douglas, Isle of Man
Lune to Morecambe Bay and Fleetwood
Belle to Southport and Liverpool
Lune to Fleetwood, return by train or tram
Bickerstaffe to Southport and Liverpool
Greyhound to Fleetwood and Morecambe Bay cruise
Greyhound to Liverpool

From North Pier:-
Greyhound to Llandudno, Bangor and Menai Bridge
Wellington to Fleetwood and Morecambe Bay Cruise
Queen of the North to Douglas, Isle of Man
Greyhound to Fleetwood, return by train or tram

One hour pleasure cruises were also advertised at both piers, *Belle*, *Lune*, *Wellington* or *Bickerstaffe* were the vessels usually employed for these cruises. These short cruise sailings had been introduced at Blackpool nearly 30 years earlier by the little Fleetwood registered paddle-steamer *Dhu Heartach* built on Tyneside by Wigham Richardson in 1868. The steamer was brought to Blackpool in 1876 by Alderman W. H. Cocker, Blackpool's first Mayor. The vessel was sold to Southport ownership in 1884. Other pleasure steamers which operated at Blackpool in later years included the ex-Mersey ferry *Minden* (ex-*Bidston*) brought to Blackpool in 1933 and *Queen of the Bay*, acquired in 1935. Both these vessels were sold in 1937. The last steamer to operate the summer seasons at the resort was the Glasgow registered *Atalanta*.

At Fleetwood a new company, The Fleetwood Steam Pleasure Boat Company, was formed in 1900 to operate steamship trips out of Fleetwood with the little screw steamer *Pioneer* which served until 1905. Also at Fleetwood the railway company paddle steamer *Lune* and the two tugs *Fylde* and *Cleveleys* offered summer-season trips from the port. In August, 1907, these little steamers between them carried thousands of sightseers to view the Royal Navy's Channel Fleet – 14 warships which anchored in the Lune Deeps of Morecambe Bay during the course of a courtesy cruise around Britain. *Lune* was sold to Messrs. Cosens of Weymouth in 1913 who re-named the ship *Melcombe Regis*, the vessel was eventually scrapped in 1923. From Heysham the Midland Railway's *Wyvern* was a regular caller in Fleetwood with daily sailings between Heysham, Morecambe, Fleetwood and Blackpool. Also from Heysham came the little steamer *Roses* which had been built for the Morecambe Steam Boat Company in 1876 and the steamship *Robina* owned by the Morecambe Central Pier Company.

An innovation at Fleetwood in 1906 was the introduction of petrol engined motor launches built by Messrs Arral Johnson at Paisley and owned by the Fylde Motor Service Company. These 35ft (10.75m) boats *Ian* and *Angus* operated for only two years at Fleetwood. The Company went out of business in 1908 after failing.

Local boatmen still operate at Fleetwood today and, all year round, sea-angling trips are a regular feature on Fleetwood's riverside scene and the same boatmen offer pleasure cruises in the summer season.

The Paddle Steamer *Bickerstaffe* crowded with day-trippers.

Bickerstaffe was built by Messrs. Laird Bros at Birkenhead for Robert and John Bickerstaffe of Blackpool and the ship was registered at Fleetwood on 22nd May, 1879. In 1894 ownership passed to the Blackpool Passenger Steamboat Company, the principal shareholder of which was John Bickerstaffe. This 155ft (48m) paddle steamer was very successful throughout its years at the resort (in 1917 the Admiralty took the vessel for service as a mine-sweeper during World War 1, the ship returning in time for the 1919 summer season) and was always popular with the holiday-makers. *Bickerstaffe* was finally taken out of service in 1928 to be scrapped at Garston.

The Fleetwood registered paddle steamer *Queen of the North*.

Built by Laird Bros. at Birkenhead for the Blackpool Passenger Steamboat Company to provide day-excursions to the Isle of Man, *Queen of the North* entered service in June, 1895. The steamer was time-tabled to sail from Blackpool at 9.30am arriving at Douglas at 1 o'clock. After a 3.5 hour stay, the ship set out on her return journey at 4.30pm. On occasions when adverse sea conditions prevented her from landing at a Blackpool pier, the ship berthed at Fleetwood, the passengers going on to Blackpool by train or by tram. On wartime service with the Royal Navy during World War 1, *Queen of the North* was lost on 20th July 1917, mined off Orford Ness.

Minden.

This former Mersey ferry was acquired by Blackpool Pleasure Steamers Limited in 1933. Built at West Hartlepool as *Bidston* in 1903, the vessel worked on the Liverpool – Birkenhead Woodside ferry service until 1932. Renamed *Minden* she then sailed from Blackpool's North Pier and, as with other pleasure steamers, Fleetwood was a frequent port of call on her excursions. The ship was sold in 1937 and broken up at Preston in 1938.

Atalanta, Blackpool's last Pleasure Steamer.

The 486 gross tons triple-screw steamer was owned by the Blackpool Steam Navigation Company, purchased by them in 1937. *Atalanta* was built by John Brown & Co. at Clydebank for the Glasgow & South Western Railway Company in 1906. The railway company used her for their popular excursion sailings and later she was the regular vessel employed to operate the ferry service between Ardrossan and the Isle of Arran. Brought to Blackpool, *Atalanta* was again engaged as an excursion steamer during the 1938 and 1939 seasons but this role ended with the onset of war in September 1939. Taken by the navy, *Atalanta* served as a Boom Defence Vessel until 1945 and when war ended she was scrapped at Methil. In this photograph the ship is seen in happier days sailing up the Wyre to Fleetwood with a good crowd of day-trippers.

(Continued on page 85)

The Sail Training Ship *Lord Nelson*.

Reminicent of Fleetwood's early years, when sailing ships of every type sailed up the River Wyre to bring their cargoes into port, the Barque *Lord Neslon* was photographed in 1989 as she sailed into Fleetwood to make a 'Voyage crew' change. The ship is owned and operated by the Jubilee Sailing Trust and was built in Cook's yard, Wivenhoe and launched in 1984. Designed and built to take disabled people to sea, there are lifts available between decks and gangways and doors accommodate wheelchairs. A permanent crew of ten staff the vessel together with a voyage crew of 40, half of whom would be physically handicapped. Photo. P.Horsley.

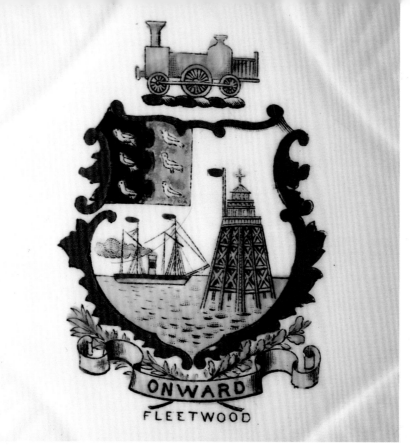

Fleetwood's original badge reflecting the town's beginnings as a railway seaport.

First used as the shield of the Fleetwood Town Commissioners, who acted as the Local Authority from 1842 until 1894, the badge bears the Martlets from the Arms of Sir Peter Hesketh-Fleetwood together with representations of an early steamship, the original Wyre Light which guided ships to the port, and an early Lancashire & Yorkshire Railway engine with its typical "Haystack" firebox. In 1894 Fleetwood Urban District Council was formed, they adopted the Commissioners' badge and added the motto "Onward". This photograph is of the badge depicted on chinaware presented to mark the formation of the Urban District Council in 1894.

When Fleetwood was incorporated as a Borough in 1933 a new Coat-of-Arms was designed to reflect the town's wider civic status but the motto "Onward" was retained. Photo by P. Horsley.

The caustic-soda tanker *Silver Kestrel*.

Built at Norrkoping in 1965, *Silver Kestrel* was first operated by the Cornhill Shipping Company Limited and was then a frequent visitor to Fleetwood. Owned and operated later by Silver Chemical Tankers Limited of London, she continued to visit the port regularly but the ship was sold in 1975. Renamed *Carrick Kestrel* and later *Goldcrest* in Bahamas registry, the vessel has continued in service into the 1990's but has not docked at Fleetwood. Photo. P.Horsley.

Danish sisters at Fleetwood.

In June, 1972 the Danish owned sister-ships *Tovelil* and *Roselil* met at Fleetwood. Whilst *Tovelil* was loading scrap for Spain *Roselil* arrived with a cargo of potatoes and berthed astern of her sister. Both vessels were owned by A.N. Sverrer Partredei and were registered at Esbjerg, Denmark. Photo. P.Horsley.

Argo Pioneer being rotated in Wyre Dock, November 1979.

Built at Perama by the Argo Shipbuilding & Repairing Company in 1976 and under the Greek flag, the vessel measured 1578 gross tons and had a length of 80 metres. Berthed at the grain silo wharf is the Panamanian registered, *Neuwulmstorf*, built at Kure, in Japan in 1977. Photo. P.Horsley.

The *M.V. Bothniaborg* sailing light up the Wyre Channel in July, 1978.

Bothniaborg was brought to Fleetwood to load a 2400 ton cargo of scrap metal for shipment to Spain. The Dutch registered 1577 gross tons general cargo vessel was owned and operated by Wagenborg of Rotterdam. Photo. by P.Horsley.

Whitehaven's coal-fired steam dredger *Clearway*.

Photographed in 1979 looking very smart in a new coat of paint, *Clearway* had been to Fleetwood for survey, new bottom doors and repainting. Built by Alexander Hall & Company in 1927 for the Whitehaven Harbour Commissioners, the little Aberdeen built grab-dredger is thought to have been the last coal-fired vessel to have been employed in Britain. The ship can still be seen, 'moth-balled' now, in Whitehaven's dock. Photo. by P.Horsley.

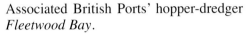

Associated British Ports' hopper-dredger *Fleetwood Bay*.

Built in Aveiro, Portugal, as *Atria* in 1980 this 1106 gross tons dredger was bought by A.B.P. in 1983 for service at Fleetwood and named *Fleetwood Bay*. The ship worked at the port until 1989 when she was sold to French owners at Dunkirk and renamed *La Flandre*. Photo. P.Horsley.

The Royal National Lifeboat Institution's *Ann Letitia Russell*.

Ann Letitia Russell, Fleetwood's Lifeboat from 1939-1976, photographed as she was launched down the slipway from the Lifeboat Station in 1951. Photo. by Colin Lynch.

RNLB. *Fisherman's Friend.*

Largely funded from a sponsored fundraising scheme initiated by the local firm Lofthouse of Fleetwood Ltd., makers of the famous Fisherman's Friend products, the lifeboat *Fisherman's Friend* was named and dedicated at a ceremony in Fleetwood's yacht marina in June, 1993. Manning the new Mersey class boat for the ceremony were members of the Fleetwood lifeboat crew. *Fisherman's Friend* is presently serving in the Royal National Lifeboat Institution's reserve fleet. Photo. P.Horsley.

Dawn light at the Fish-dock, 1966.

Viewed from beneath the Fish-market canopy, the camera has framed the Motor Trawler *Dorinda* (J. Marr & Son) picked out in the first light of dawn and mirrored in the still water of the dock. The funnel, engine-room casing and davit of the Steam Trawler *Imperialist* (Wyre Trawlers Ltd.) outline the picture. Photo. P.Horsley.

Royalist.

Few colour photographs of a working trawler built as early as 1911 can have been taken, but seen here is the Hewett Fishing Company's *Royalist*, launched at Selby in 1911. The trawler had a long and varied career. Built for the Western Steam Trawling Company of Bristol as the *Alnmouth*, the ship was first registered at Bristol in 1912 with the fishing number BL15. Purchased by the Admiralty in 1914 the trawler served throughout the 1914-1918 War as *HMT. Alnmouth*, Pennant number FY12, and then in 1919 was sold to Vulcan Trawlers Limited of Fleetwood and had the fishing number FD335. In 1927 the ship was again sold and transferred to Aberdeen (fishing number A196). Sold again in 1932 to French owners at Dieppe the trawler was there renamed *La Manche*. In 1935 the vessel passed to her last owners, Hewetts, as *Royalist* and fished out of Fleetwood until being scrapped in July, 1960. Registered at London, as were all the Hewett vessels, *Royalist* took the fishing number L090. After 25 years the company made plans to replace her with a modern diesel engined trawler which was to carry on the name and so briefly, in 1960, the old steam trawler became *Royalist II* just before going to the breakers' yard at Preston after a working life of almost half a century.

Motor Trawler *Armana*.

Armana FD207 was built at Goole in 1962 for the Fleetwood Trawler owners J.Marr & Son, a fine 437 gross tons diesel engined vessel. The trawler fished out of Fleetwood until 1969 when she was sold to South African ownership and, in 1994, was still fishing out of Cape Town. Photo. by P.Horsley.

Boston Blenheim.

Boston Deep-sea Fisheries' stern-trawler *Boston Blenheim* FD137, built at Hessle in 1971 and photographed leaving Fleetwood for the fishing grounds in 1974. Photo. by P.Horsley.

Pandoro Ferries' *Ibex*.

Ibex in light-blue livery during her spell on the Fleetwood-Larne route and viewed from mid-river at low water. Photo. P.Horsley.

The bow-loading *Skarvoy* at Fleetwood's Ro-Ro berth in 1989.

Built as *Fernbay* in 1974 and then named *Gardenia* before becoming *Skarvoy*, the vessel was again renamed in 1993 to become *African Trailer*. Photo. P.Horsley.

Puma.

Pandoro's Ro-Ro vehicle ferry *Puma* (ex. *Union Melbourne*), in service on the Fleetwood-Larne route.

Mona's Queen arriving at Fleetwood in the late evening to be ready for what was to be the last sailing of the daily Isle of Man summer services which were ended in 1961. A nostalgic photograph looking over the Amusements lights and the Open-air swimming pool, now long gone, as the Isle of Man steamer glides along a glassy sea for the final service out of Fleetwood. Photo. by P.Horsley.

Mona's Isle setting sail for Douglas on Wednesday, 25th August 1971 when, after a ten year gap, the Isle of Man Steam Packet Company restored a limited service of summer excursion sailings from Fleetwood. Photo. P.Horsley.

Seacat Isle of Man.

The modern Seacat introduced to the Isle of Man Steam Packet Company's fleet in 1994 made her first passenger service for the Company on the Fleetwood - Douglas route. Built by International Catamarans in Hobart, Tasmania in 1989 the vessel had a cruising speed of 35 knots, max. speed 42 knots, and a capacity for 400 passengers and 80 cars. The Seacat had previously served as *Hoverspeed France* and as *Seacat Boulogne* before being chartered to the Steam Packet. *Seacat Isle of Man* operated the excursion sailings to the Island for the 1994 and 1995 seasons but the Seacat is to be replaced by a larger 'Fast Craft'. In the meantime the 1996 excursion sailings have again been served by the *Lady of Mann*. Photograph by P. Horsley.

"Fun Boat" excursions.

Mona's Queen illuminated by the setting sun as she sailed back into Fleetwood at the end of a summer-season 'Fun Boat' excursion to the Isle of Man. Photograph by P. Horsley.

S.S. *Pioneer* owned by the Fleetwood Steam Pleasure Boat Company.

Pioneer was built by Messrs. Monk & Son at Preston in 1899 to operate as a pleasure steamer at Lytham and Southport but the 72 foot, 45 gross tons steamship was purchased by the Fleetwood company in 1900 for the sum of £1,900. The little steamer had a well furnished saloon cabin to accommodate 80 passengers and a Board of Trade Certificate for 255 persons. *Pioneer* sailed from the landing stage on Fleetwood's ferry beach to the Wardley's Hotel some 4 miles upriver where a wooden landing pier had been built in 1899 in readiness for this trade, the Hotel providing refreshment and entertainment for the excursion trippers. Cruises to the Wyre Light and to Morecambe were also operated. The enterprise failed to achieve the profitability anticipated by the promoters and came to an end in 1905, *Pioneer* being sold to new owners in Torquay. Ownership of the vessel changed again in 1916 when the ship went to Pembroke Dock and *Pioneer* was eventually broken up in 1935.

The twin-screw Heysham steam tug-tender *Wyvern*.

Built by Ferguson Bros of Port Glasgow in 1905 as the Heysham Harbour tug, the 215 tons *Wyvern* was always intended by her owners, the Midland Railway Company, for dual use and was designed with ample passenger accommodation. Midland Railway put a brand-new fast steamer, *Manxman*, on the Heysham - Douglas route to compete with and outsail the Isle of Man Steam Packet Company's ships sailing out of Fleetwood. *Wyvern* immediately commenced a Heysham-Fleetwood service deliberately time-tabled to poach Isle of Man passengers from Fleetwood. Touts canvassed passengers waiting to board the Fleetwood-Douglas packets advising them that by transferring to Heysham on *Wyvern* and boarding *Manxman* they could be in Douglas before the Fleetwood ship. This was "Fighting Talk" to the I.O.M.S.P. Company who promptly brought the even faster *Viking* to Fleetwood to beat off the competition. Over the years, *Wyvern* continued to operate passenger services and excursions between Heysham, Fleetwood and Blackpool and to work as the harbour tug at Heysham until being taken out of service in 1959 and then scrapped.

Chapter 7

Fleetwood & the
Barrow-in-Furness Route
"The Barrow Boats"

Services from Fleetwood to the northern shores of Morecambe Bay began in 1840 when Sir Peter Hesketh-Fleetwood's own paddle-steamers *James Dennistoun*, *Cupid* and *Express* set up regular sailings to Bardsea, the landing place for Ulverston. The paddle-steamers *Fireking* and *Victoria* are also recorded as having been in service on this route. Barrow-in-Furness did not then exist other than as a cluster of cottages, the town and port there came later after the extension of the Furness Railway. In 1846 Piel Pier was built and the daily service from Fleetwood to Bardsea became a Fleetwood to Piel (Barrow) service operated by the paddle-steamer *Ayrshire Lassie*. In 1848 and 1849 the Liverpool, Fleetwood and Furness Steam Packet Company took over the route operating a service from Piel to Liverpool via Fleetwood using the paddle-steamer *Zephyr* and, again, *James Dennistoun* chartered from the Birkenhead & Chester Railway who by then owned the vessel. The service lapsed but in 1856 *Helvellyn* was put on the route by the Barrow Steam Navigation Co. and operated between Barrow and Fleetwood until 1876 after which the service again lapsed, apart from irregular excursion trips from Blackpool and Fleetwood by various pleasure steamers including *Wellington*, *Bickerstaffe* and *Lune*.

The service between Barrow and Fleetwood which came to be popularly known as "The Barrow Boats" began in 1900. The carriage of iron ores by the Furness Railway began to tail off as local ore deposits were worked out. This trade had, until the turn of the century, provided most of the Furness Railway Company's income. In order to boost their finances the Railway Company sought to develop their passenger traffic and decided to run a summer season steamer service to Fleetwood to tap into the booming holiday trade generated by Blackpool. Inclusive bookings from Blackpool to the Lakes via Fleetwood and a

steamer crossing to Barrow were introduced. A paddle-steamer, *Lady Evelyn*, was built for the new service in 1900 and the route between Fleetwood and Barrow proved extremely popular. The first year sailings in 1900 were advertised as :-

From Ramsden Dock, Barrow... 7.0 am.   3.15pm. and 6.0pm.
Departures from Fleetwood... 9.15am   4.50pm. and 10.45pm.

... the return fare for the steamer crossing was 3 shillings (15p).

A second paddle-steamer, *Lady Margaret*, was purchased from P & A Campbell's fleet to augment the service in 1903. Built by A.MacMillan & Son at Dumbarton in 1896, the vessel had served on Bristol Channel routes prior to joining the Furness Railway fleet. At 210ft(64m) and 369 gross tons, *Lady Margaret* was larger and faster then her predecessor and remained on the service until being sold to the Admiralty in 1908. Sailings on the Fleetwood - Barrow route continued, *Philomel* was brought to the route to replace *Lady Margaret* and in 1909 the *Lady Moyra* was added to the Furness Railway fleet. When war came in 1914 the service was cancelled when the ships went to the Royal Navy. When peace came in 1918 the Fleetwood - Barrow service was not restored, the Company's two remaining ships, *Lady Evelyn* and *Lady Moyra* were sold after their release by the Admiralty.

Lady Evelyn.

Built by J. Scott & Son at Kinghorn, Fifeshire, in 1900 for the Furness Railway Company, the paddle steamer *Lady Evelyn* established the successful service between Fleetwood and Barrow which operated from 1900 until the outbreak of war in 1914. This 342 gross tons vessel was lengthened to 200feet (61m) in 1904 to give a passenger capacity for 714 persons. In Royal Navy service as a mine-sweeper throughout the 1914 - 1918 War, *Lady Evelyn* was sold in 1918 after her return to the Railway Company and operated on Bristol Channel routes. Acquired later by P & A Campbell, the ship was renamed *Brighton Belle* and transferred to their South coast fleet. Later, again in Admiralty service on 28th.May 1940, during the Dunkirk evacuation operations, *Brighton Belle* struck submerged wreckage and was lost.

Philomel.

Purchased by the Furness Railway Company in 1907 as a replacement for the *Lady Margaret*, the 564 tons Paddle Steamer *Philomel* had been built for the General Steam Navigation Company in 1889 and had operated as one of that Company's River Thames steamers. *Philomel*, usually referred to as the "Full-o-smell" by regular travellers served on the Fleetwood - Barrow crossing until 1913 when the vessel was withdrawn from service and broken-up at Preston.

Lady Moyra.

Bought by the Railway Company in 1910, *Lady Moyra* was the fastest steamer to serve on the Fleetwood - Barrow route and, though able to make the crossing in 45 minutes, her normal service time was 1 hour. Built as *Gwalia* in 1905 for the Barry Railway Company, the steamer had operated on the Barry - Cardiff - Ilfracombe route until her acquisition by the Furness Railway. Re-named *Lady Moyra* after a daughter of the Cavendish family, as were all three of the "LADY" ships owned by the Furness Railway, the vessel was sold together with *Lady Evelyn* after the 1914 - 1918 War and as *Brighton Queen* she was, like her companion ship, lost during the Dunkirk evacuation, bombed and disabled by enemy aircraft on 1st June,1940 and eventually shelled and sunk by enemy gunfire.

Chapter 8

Ferry Across the Wyre
The Knott End Ferries

Prior to the making of the town and port of Fleetwood in the 1830s there was little call for ferrying across the mouth of the River Wyre itself. A long established passenger ferry was operated across the river a few miles upstream at Wardleys where a boatman at Cockle Hall on the Old Thornton bank obliged would-be passengers when called upon. At Shard, close by the present day Shard Bridge, a gravel bed enabled cart and carriage traffic to ford the Wyre at low water thus linking the old town of Poulton with the Over-Wyre districts. The area now covered by the spread of Fleetwood was then a sandy waste, the principal residents of which were colonies of sea-birds and numerous rabbits. Such occasional travellers who did seek to cross the river at its mouth called on the services of the Croft and the Ainsworth families, fishermen and river pilots who lived in the riverside cottages of "Sea Dyke" and "Spring Bank" on the Knott End side of the river.

The establishing of Fleetwood changed everything. The growing population of Fleetwood gave employment to some people from the rural areas across the Wyre. Farmers and cottagers from Preesall, Pilling and the outlying hamlets brought their produce to the market created by the ever growing population settling at Fleetwood. Migrant workers from Lancaster, Garstang and North Lancashire arrived at Knott End seeking to cross to Fleetwood. The Knott End fishermen built up a thriving business as ferrymen and owned many small rowing and sailing boats working the ferry crossing and, later, also operating summer-season pleasure boats sailing river trips and excursions in Morecambe Bay, popular pastimes with Victorian visitors. The ferrymen were able to hire a steam-yacht, the *Glory,* for these excursions during the 1880s and used her also to augment the ferry service when needed. *Success, Quail, Nymph, Playfair* and *Guarantee,* the latter two converted as steam launches, were some of the Croft's boats regularly used for the ferry service. The largest boat built for the ferrymen was the steam-ferry *Onward.*

The Local Council gained the right to operate the ferry services in 1893 and at first John Croft continued the service under Licence of the Fleetwood Urban District Council. In 1898 the Council itself took over the ferry operation, *Onward* and a smaller boat were purchased from the Crofts and Mr Thomas Croft was appointed as ferry Manager for the Council. The Authority developed the ferry service by adding more steamers and a regular time-tabled, all year round service was instituted. *Progress,* a 52ft twin-screw wooden hulled steam ferry was built for the service in 1899 by local shipwrights John Gibson & Son, a little steamer which remained in service until 1930. *Bourne May* came from the same shipbuilder in 1901. The ferry undertaking thrived and, though in service year-round for the many Knott-End and Preesall residents commuting across the river and for carrying mails, newspapers and local deliveries, the summer holiday visitors made up the bulk of the passenger traffic and generated most of the undertaking's income. In 1905, records show that on 14th August, a bank holiday, 10,200 passengers crossed the river on that one day alone. The ferry service continued as a profitable venture for the next 50 years and new vessels were introduced as older boats were scrapped. *Pilling,* the first motor vessel in the fleet was purchased in 1920 and served as the low-water ferry until 1941. The Pride of the fleet, *Wyresdale* was built in 1924, *Lunevale* joined in 1935 and the *Caldervale* was bought in 1941. The corporation's last ferry boat, *Viking 66,* was built for the service in 1966.

From the 1950s onwards the profitability of the service declined and ultimately had to be heavily subsidised, first by Fleetwood Corporation and then by Lancashire County Council. The operating of the ferry service was eventually contracted out by the Local Authority to private operators and now "The wheel has gone full circle", once again local boatmen provide the ferry across the Wyre.

Knott End ferry boat *Guarantee*.

John, James and Robert Croft of Knott End owned and operated the little steam launch *Guarantee*, licenced to carry 29 persons, one of their fleet of small boats used for the Fleetwood-Knott End ferry service. When Fleetwood Urban District Council took over the running of the ferry operation in 1898 *Guarantee* and her sister *Playfair*, each minus its engine and boiler, were purchased by the Council for £28 the pair.

Ferry Steamer *Onward*.

Built at Fleetwood by John Gibson & Sons in 1888 for the Knott End ferrymen, *Onward* was purchased by the Fleetwood Council in 1898 for the sum of £938. The 50ft (15m) 19 tons boat was rebuilt and a new engine installed in 1900 when a new licence was granted for 135 passengers.

The ferry boat *Bourne May* linked Fleetwood and Knott End for 43 years.

Built at Fleetwood in 1901 by John Gibson and Sons and engined by the local engineering firm of James Robertson & Sons Ltd., the twin screw *Bourne May* served until February 1944. At 25 tons, length 58 ft (17.7m) the ferry was larger than her predecessors and had good below deck accommodation for winter travellers. The ferry took the name of the Bourne family of Stalmine Hall the last of whom, Miss Harriet Bourne, married Mr James W May who added his wife's name to his own and brought his wealth to that of the Bournes to become a prominent local benefactor.

Fleetwood Corporation's ferry-boat *Wyresdale*.

Built for Fleetwood Corporation's Knott End ferry service in 1924 *Wyresdale* was the largest ferry to maintain the link across the Wyre. Licensed for 250 passengers the *Wyresdale* was a comfortable ferry popular with summer visitors and winter commuters alike, she had a warm saloon for winter and ample deck space for trippers.

Lunevale.

The twin-screw diesel engined *Lunevale* was built for Fleetwood Corporation by Yarwood's of Northwich in 1935. Certificated for 230 passengers, the ferry worked the Fleetwood-Knott End service until 1966.

Motor ferry *Caldervale.*

Built at Conway, North Wales, as *Queen Elizabeth* in 1937, the vessel was purchased by Fleetwood Corporation in 1941 for the ferry service and renamed *Caldervale*. Originally powered by petrol/paraffin engines, new Russell-Newbury diesels were fitted in 1949. The boat operated on the Wyre crossing until 1966.

Viking 66.

Designed and built specifically for Fleetwood Corporation's ferry service, the ferry boat was delivered in 1966 at a cost of £8,000. Plagued by breakdown and damage and, on one occasion, hijacked by a would-be ocean traveller who succeeded only in stranding the vessel some miles along the Fylde coast, *Viking 66* had a chequered career and was eventually sold after a survey in 1987 revealed that repairs costing £20,000 were needed.

Knott End ferry, 1993.

After nearly ninety years of operation by the local authority, the ferry service across the River Wyre was contracted out to private operators. Pictured here in 1993, local boatmen provide the ferry service as in the years prior to 1898.

Chapter 9

Docks and harbour vessels

Many 'unsung' working vessels contribute to the day-to-day operation of an active seaport. At Fleetwood, dredgers and hoppers have been of particular importance for the Wyre has always been subject to heavy silting. From the port's earliest days dredgers, the first one brought into action in 1840, were used to maintain a sufficient depth of water at the quays and steamer berths. When the enclosed dock was constructed a man-made channel was excavated to link the lock-pit to the river and over the years constant work by dredgers was needed to retain access to the dock. In early years bucket-dredgers, served by a mini-fleet of spoil-hoppers, were employed. Later, suction-dredger/hopper vessels continued the task. The port's last bucket dredger was sold in 1963. Dredging costs increased and at the same time commercial traffic to Fleetwood declined, even the mainstay fishing activity 'nosedived' after the 'Cod-Wars' and eventually the port operators (Associated British Ports) brought their own dredging activities to an end. P & O Ferries assumed responsibility for keeping clear the Wyre approach and the areas at the RoRo berth and its turning circle. Silting has affected the channel leading to the enclosed dock but some drag-dredging has kept the passage clear for yachts and small fishing vessels. Moves to bring larger trawlers back to Fleetwood have increased the dredging effort and recently the Heysham dredger *Ogmore* has worked at the dock.

Tug boats have been busy at Fleetwood from the port's early days. Tugs brought the larger sailing vessels in and out of the dock and harbour and by 1887 the towing rates were established as:-

Coasting vessels, to and from Wyre Light, 3d(£0.0125p) per ton
Foreign vessels, to and from Wyre Light, 3 guineas (£3.15p)
Foreign vessels, beyond Danger Patch, 3 guineas per hour.
Foreign vessels towing from sea and docking same tide, 3d per ton.

As Fleetwood grew as a seaside resort, most of the port's tugs had a dual role in the summer providing pleasure trips and excursions. *Lune*, the port's last paddle-tug, was used to handle the large sailing ships which brought their cargoes to Fleetwood but was also a busy pleasure steamer with splendid passenger accommodation and well appointed saloon. The port's operators retained tugs at Fleetwood until 1969 when towage provision was undertaken by the then chief users, the Fleetwood Fishing Vessel Owners' Association.

Other work boats at the port have served as tenders and harbour launches, pilot boats and buoy vessels. *Robin* served for many years as the trawler-owners' tender and the local fish-oil works had a succession of small boats - *Isaco*, *Wisteria* and, lastly, *Seamaid* which collected liver-oil and fish offal from the trawlers. Associated British Ports Limited keep *Wyre Surveyor* as the current harbour launch and buoy vessel at Fleetwood.

Fleet List. Fleetwood Dredgers & Hoppers

To F'wood	Vessel	Built	Gross Tons	Length Ft/m	Notes
1840	A 20.h.p. SteamDredger	Launched at Fleetwood. 21st Jan, 1840			Built for Sir Peter Hesketh Fleetwood and owned later by the Preston & Wyre Railway, Harbour & Dock Co.
1875	Fleetwood (I)	W.Simons & Co. Ltd. Renfrew, 1872	122	82 25m	Steam bucket-dredger for Preston & Wyre Railway, later L&YR. Sold to Belfast owners in 1907 as Dundrum, later to Whitehaven.
1881	Rossall (I)	Barrow S.B.&E Co. Barrow. 1881.	192	112 34m	Steam Lighter/Spoil Barge. Iron hull twin-screw steamer. Transferred to Widnes in 1913, scrapped 1920.
1893	Blackpool	Murdock & Murray, Port Glasgow, 1893.	293	129.7 39.5m	Twin-screw steam hopper, scrapped 1944.
1894	Lytham	Murdock & Murray, Port Glasgow, 1894.	292	129 39.3m	Twin-screw steam hopper, transferred to Barrow in 1936 and scrapped in March, 1947.
1896	Kirkham	Murdock & Murray. Port Glasgow, 1896.	319	136 41.5m	Twin-screw steam hopper, scrapped in May, 1937.
1898	Neptune	W.Simons & Co. Ltd Renfrew, 1881.	312	145 44.2m	Twin-screw self propelled bucket-dredger. Scrapped in January, 1937.
1899	Poulton	Flemming & Ferguson Paisley, 1899.	1072	204 62m	Twin-screw steam suction dredger/hopper. Scrapped in 1957.
1906	Fleetwood (II)	Ferguson Bros., Port Glasgow, 1906.	479	166 50.6m	Single-screw self-propelled bucket-dredger. Scrapped in 1937.
1912	Preesall	W.Simons & Co.Ltd. Renfrew, 1912.	572	165 50.3m	Twin-screw steam-hopper, scrapped in 1963.
1921	Rossall (II)	Olderfleet S.B.Co. Larne, 1920.	239	107 32.6m	Single-screw steam grab-dredger, ship's name Nellie when built. Sold in 1950, scrapped in 1976.
1936	Fylde (III)	W.Simons & Co. Ltd. Renfrew, 1936.	465	176 53.6m	Self-winching dumb-barge bucket dredger. Sold in 1963.
1947	Dalmeny	C.H.Walker, Sudbrook, 1914.	472	166.5 50.7m	Single-screw steam hopper acquired by the L&NW Railway at Garston Docks, 1921. To Fleetwood in 1947, scrapped in 1963.
1960	Queensferry	C.H.Walker, Sudbrook, 1914.	472	166.5 50.7m	Single-screw steam hopper, sister ship to Dalmeny, relief at Fleetwood in 1960 and scrapped in 1963.
1961	"G"	H.Robb & Son Ltd. Leith, 1927.	591	170.1 33.7m	Single-screw steam hopper. Sold to J.Carney & Sons, Sunderland in 1964. Renamed Carnside.
1962	Bleasdale	Simons-Lobenitz. Renfrew, 1962.	1029	193 58.8m	Diesel-Electric trailing suction dredger/hopper built for service at Fleetwood. Scrapped in 1982.
1974	Grassendale	H.Scarr Ltd. Hessle, 1954.	677	165 50.3m	Motor Vessel. Normally based at Barrow, regularly in service at Fleetwood to clear the enclosed dock. Grab-dredger/hopper.
1983	Fleetwood Bay	Aveiro, Portugal in 1980.	1106	181.5 55m	ex Atria. Sold to French ownership in 1989 and renamed as La Flandre. Suction dredger/hopper.
1990	Mersey Venture	Appledore S.B. Co. in 1983.	2647	272 82.4m	Twin-screw Motor Vessel. Suction dredger/hopper on contract to Pandoro Ferries dredging the Wyre Channel and Ro-Ro berthing.

Excavating the Wyre Dock channel in 1876.

The lock giving access to the Wyre Dock is linked to the river by a man-made channel seen here being excavated in 1876. The bucket-dredger *Fleetwood* can be seen working to deepen the trenching of the construction gangs. The dredger, built in 1875 at a cost of £12,000, was powered by a 100 h.p. steam engine, was capable of raising 250 tons of spoil per hour and could work to a depth of 26 feet (7.9m).

Bucket-dredger *Neptune* at work.

Originally owned by the Lancashire & Yorkshire Railway Company from 1881, ownership was vested jointly to the L&Y R/London & NW Railways at Fleetwood in 1898. The vessel was powered by two inverted vertical compound engines and had boilers supplied by the Naval Construction & Armaments Co. of Barrow-in-Furness. The *Neptune* worked at Fleetwood until 1937.

Poulton, Fleetwood's first suction dredger.

The trailing suction-dredger/hopper *Poulton* was the first dredger of this type to work at the port and remained in service for nearly 58 years. Built by Flemming and Ferguson at Paisley in 1899, *Poulton* was scrapped at Preston in 1957.

Steam hopper *Preesall*.

The steam hopper barge *Preesall* was the last of the spoil-hoppers to be ordered for service at Fleetwood. Built by Simon & Co. at Renfrew in 1912, *Preesall* was brought to the port to augment her three smaller predecessors *Blackpool*, *Lytham*, and *Kirkham*, each of which had come from the yards of Messrs. Murdock & Murray at Port Glasgow. *Preesall* remained in service at Fleetwood until 1963.

Fylde III Fleetwood's last bucket dredger.

Another Railway owned vessel which had come from the yards of Simon & Co. at Renfrew and built in 1936 for the London, Midland & Scottish Railway, the then owners of Fleetwood Docks. *Fylde* was a non-self-propelled (dumb barge) bucket-dredger which was usually manoeuvered about the harbour and the Dock-channel by one of the harbour tugs, but could also winch itself along the quaysides. In the evening's quiet or early in the morning the clanking of the bucket dredger at work could be heard all over the town. Sold in 1963, the vessel is reported to be still at work, converted to diesel power but otherwise largely original and clearing silt in the inland water ways of the Netherlands

Hopper-barge 'G' at Fleetwood in 1961.

Between the scrapping of the port's suction dredger *Poulton* in 1957 and the arrival of the replacement vessel *Bleasdale* in 1962, various grab dredgers and hoppers brought from other ports were employed at Fleetwood. Here the steam hopper 'G' was photographed moored along-side the bucket dredger *Fylde* in the "Ballast Corner" of Wyre Dock. 'G' had previously been in service at Garston docks and after her spell of employment at Fleetwood was sold to Sunderland shipowners who renamed her *Carnside*. Photo. by P.Horsley.

The single-screw steam hopper-barge *Queensferry* at Fleetwood in 1962.

The steam hoppers *Dalmeny* and *Queensferry* were sister ships built in 1914. Both were acquired by the Railway Company for service in the Mersey/Garston Section and both, too, were also in service at Fleetwood. *Dalmeny* was transferred to Fleetwood as early as 1947 and she was joined by her sister-ship in 1962. Both vessels were scrapped in 1963. Photo. by P.Horsley.

Grassendale, a grab-dredger normally employed at Barrow and Silloth.

The 677 tons motor vessel *Grassendale*, built 1954 and owned then by the British Transport Docks Board, came frequently to Fleetwood in the late 1950's and early 1960's to work in the river and dock channels prior to the arrival of the *Bleasdale* in 1962. After that date the grab-dredger was occasionally brought into Fleetwood docks to clear the corners not normally accessible to a suction dredger. Another vessel from Barrow which worked at Fleetwood was the grab-dredger *Rhymney*. Photo. by P.Horsley.

Bleasdale, suction dredger/hopper built for service at Fleetwood.

Built by Simons-Lobnitz Ltd. for the British Transport Docks Board in 1962, the 1029 gross tons *Bleasdale* was a Diesel-electric vessel fitted with a bow-thruster system. For twenty years the ship worked at the port clearing the Wyre channel, harbour, and the Dock channel areas, a very familiar 'Work-horse' on the Fleetwood scene until her replacement in 1982 by the *Fleetwood Bay*.

The highly automated trailing suction-dredger *Mersey Venture*.

A regular visitor to the port of Fleetwood for several days each month and pictured here whilst at work along-side Fleetwood's Ro-Ro berth. Built by Appledore Shipbuilding Ltd. in 1983, the 2647 gross tons "Super-dredger" normally operates at Liverpool for the Mersey Docks and Harbour Board but is also contracted to P&O's Pandoro Ferries to routinely come to Fleetwood to keep the river channel and Ro-Ro berth area free from silting.

River Wyre gravel.

Extensive gravel beds exist in the Wyre and the river was a source of sand and gravel at various periods over the years. In the early days, barges were towed upsteam from the Harbour to be grounded as the tide ebbed. Labourers then dug and barrowed the sand and gravel to the barges until the returning tide ended their work. In the 1920's and 30's the railway company, which was the Dock Authority, themselves exploited the gravel beds using one of their older dredgers. As much as 300,000 tons of sand and gravel were recovered in one year but work at the gravel beds lapsed with the 1939-1945 War.

In 1954 the Warrington based company of James Bennett (Contractors) Ltd. resumed the working of the Wyre gravel deposits and *Wyrecrete*, a former tug converted as a barge-towing, sand-pump was engaged. A screening and washing plant was sited on the West side of the Wyre Dock lock. Kierby & Perry Ltd. also began to work the river deposits and the Fleetwood Sand and Gravel Company was formed. Two old coasters converted as dredgers, *Bretherdale* (built 1885) and *Allerdale* (built 1907) were employed to work the Fleetwood river deposits, and, lastly *Bessie Day and Pen Itchen*, from Amey Marine of Southampton, were brought to the work. The extraction of sand and gravel from the river was abandoned in 1970s as costs escalated and the enterprise ceased to be viable.

Fleetwood Sand & Gravel Company's dredger *Allerdale*, her configuration betraying her origin as a steam coaster. Built at Troon in 1907 as the 450 gross tons *Aquilla*, the ship was one of the early vessels in the fleet of the Zillah Shipping Company of Liverpool. In her final years at Fleetwood, in February 1959, *Allerdale* sank whilst berthed at the port's North-end staging, the ship rolled on her side and was submerged by the tide. Despite her age, the old steamer was successfully restored and continued to work through the 1960s. Photograph by John Bamforth.

Fleet List. Fleetwood Tugs, Tenders & Harbour Vessels

To F'wood	Vessel	Built	Gross Tons	Length Ft/m	Notes
1843	Nile	Blackwall, London in 1837.	67 bur	106/32.3m	Paddle Steamer. Wooden Hulled tug/tender owned by the Preston & Wyre Railway, Harbour & Dock Company. Sold 1854.
1854	Flying Dutchman	Sunderland, 1852	26 bur	82/25.0m	Paddle steamer. Wooden hulled tug. Owner. Frederick Kemp and later L&Y/L & NW Railways. Scrapped 1857.
1858	Adjutant	Belfast, 1858	79.5	82/25.0m	Iron hulled paddle tug. Owned by F. Kemp and others. Sold to Williams and Oulton, Liverpool, in 1866.
1862	Wyre	W.C.Miller, Liverpool in 1862	165	117/224m	Iron Hulled paddle tug owned by North Lancs. Steam Nav Co and H. Wickam Esq M.P. Sold to J McPherson, Arbroath,1892.
1870	Jabez Bunting	North Shields, 1849.	61	73/22.4m	Paddle steamer. Wooden hulled tug. Sold to J.Alsop, Preston, in 1887 and scrapped in 1893.
1881	Fylde (I)	J. Reid & Company, Port Glasgow, 1881	217	122/37m	Twin-screw tug owners L&Y/L & NW Railways. Sold to the Liverpool Salvage Assoc. in 1904. To S. Shields in 1909 as Plover.
1882	Wardleys	Murdock & Murray Ltd. Port Glasgow, 1882.	112	90/27.6m	Twin-screw tug. Sold to W.J. Guy of Cardiff in 1913 and scrapped at Cardiff in 1952.
1883	Brock	Seath & Company, Rutherglen, 1883	140	95/29m	Twin-screw tug. Sold to G.E.J. Moodie, Grimsby, 1902 then to Lawson-Batey Tugs, S. Shields as Mentor in 1904. Scrapped 1933.
1892	Lune	Seath & Company Rutherglen. 1892	252	129/39m	Paddle tug/tender with extensive passenger accommodation. Sold to Cosens & Co. Weymouth, in 1913. Renamed Melcombe Regis.
1902	Cleveleys (I)	Rennoldson & Sons South Shields, 1902	292	131/39.5m	Twin-screw steam tug. Scrapped December, 1928 at Morecambe.
1904	Fylde (II)	Ferguson Bros. Ltd. Port Glasgow, 1904	256	123/37.5m	Twin-Screw steam tug. Scrapped March, 1931.
1919	Landy (I)	Lytham S.B.& E. Co. Lytham, Lancs. 1916	51	65/18.2m	Single-Screw steam tug. Scrapped November, 1949.
1929	Cleveleys (II)	Lytham S.B.& E. Co. Lytham, Lancs. 1929	110	80/24.4m	Twin-Screw steam tug. Scrapped on Clydeside in 1969.
1938	Bispham	Denny Bros. Ltd.., Dumbarton, 1938.	21	58/17.7m	Motor vessel. Harbour tractor with Voith-Schneider propulsion system. Broken-up 1982.
1949	Landy (II)	Richard Dunston & Co. Thorne, 1949.	66	70/21.4m	Twin-screw oil engined tug owned after 1968 by Fleetwood Fishing Vessel Owners' Association. Scrapped 1974.
1968	Finch	Built, 1956	58	62/19m	ex-Boys White ex-Falconbrook. Owners – Fleetwood Fishing Vessel Owners' Association.
1981	Nicky Nook renamed Wyre Surveyor	Hancock & Lane Ltd. Daventry, Northants.	34	47/14.3m	Harbour tug/survey/buoy vessel with electronic positioning equipment for buoy maintenance etc. Owners A.B.P. Ltd.

The Joint Railways' Steam Tug *Fylde* built for Fleetwood in 1881.

After the opening of Wyre Dock in 1877 many ships came to Fleetwood, especially large sailing ships bringing grain or timber. The port's two early paddle tugs *Jabez Bunting* and *Wyre* were unable to cope with the volume of shipping then using Fleetwood. The "Joint Railways" – the Lancashire & Yorkshire Railway/London and North Western Railway – had three new twin-screw steam tugs built, *Fylde* in 1881, *Wardleys* in 1882 and *Brock* in 1883. The *Fylde*, pictured here, was sold to the Liverpool Salvage Association in 1904.

Paddle tug *Lune* shepherding a sailing ship into Wyre Dock.

The 252 ton paddle tug *Lune*, built in 1892 for service at Fleetwood, is seen here working with a large four mast barque at the entrance lock to Wyre Dock. During the summer months *Lune* was extensively employed as a pleasure steamer, a dual role for which she had been designed, having been built with ample passenger accommodation. Fleetwood's last paddle tug, *Lune* was sold in 1913 for service at Weymouth. The barque seen here is believed to be the *Lynton*.

The Steam Tug *Cleveleys*.

Built by the Lytham Shipbuilding & Engineering Company in 1929 for the L.M.S. Railway, the tug *Cleveleys* was the second tug with that name to be built for service at Fleetwood. A twin-screw vessel powered by two compound surface-condensing two cylinder engines rating 320bhp., the tug served at the port for 40 years. Pictured here in 1964 with a neat wheelhouse, the tug when built had the then more usual open bridge. Photo. by P.Horsley.

The harbour-tractor/launch *Bispham*.

An interesting little craft from W.Denny & Bros., Dumbarton, with a Gleniffer diesel unit. One of the early examples of the Voith-Schneider propulsion system to be applied, five vertical blades in a cylindrical mode were set beneath the ship's stern. Controlled feathering of various blades achieved forward, lateral, or reverse propulsion. The maker's plate on the unit carried the words and date Voith-Schneider 1939. Photo. P.Horsley.

Landy II.

Built in 1949 for the British Transport Commission, the twin-screw motor tug *Landy II* continued the name *Landy*, i.e., "L & Y" from the Lancashire & Yorkshire Railway Company's tug which had served at the port from 1919 until 1949. Pictured here in Fleetwood's Wyre Dock, the tug was purchased in 1968 by the Fleetwood Fishing Vessel Owners' Association and operated by them until being scrapped in 1974. Photo. by Ron Cox.

A tricky situation.

The harbour tug *St. Olaf* (Fleetwood Tugs Limited) and J.Marr & Son's stern-trawler *Glen Coe* both aground in the Dock channel in 1987. This little tug of 37 gross tons was built in 1956 and was originally owned by Humphrey & Grey (Lighterage) Ltd., London. Photo. by P.Horsley.

Harbour tug *Finch*.

Built as *Falconbrook* in 1956 this 310 bhp. tug was later acquired by the Thames tug operators W.E.White & Sons Ltd. in 1966 and renamed *Boys White*. Fleetwood Fishing Vessel Owners' Association purchased the vessel in 1968 for service at Fleetwood and on her arrival at the port the tug was given the name *Finch*. Photo. by Ron Cox.

M.V. Robin, for many years one of Fleetwood's most familiar harbour craft.

The little tender and harbour launch *Robin*, owned by Fleetwood Fishing Vessel Owners' Association, photographed returning to harbour after running replacement crewmen to a trawler waiting in Lune Deeps. Rather than miss a tide, trawlers sometimes had to leave port with some crew members missing. The F.F.V.O.A.s launch would then take out replacements. Built in 1936 the little 40ft (12m) motor launch served Fleetwood for 30 years and apart from duties for the trawler owners, on numerous occasions filled the role of Pilot Boat, Buoy Tender and even 'tug' for other small craft in the dock and harbour. Photo. by P.Horsley.

Nicky Nook, harbour launch and buoy vessel.

Built at Daventry, Northants, in 1981 as the replacement for the then 43 years old *Bispham*, the *Nicky Nook* came from the Engineering Company of Hancock and Lane Limited and was powered by a 170 bhp Gardner diesel. The boat was brought from Daventry by road transporter and lifted into Wyre Dock with the aid of a 160 ton crane. Fitted with the latest electronics for sounding and positioning and equipped with a $\frac{1}{2}$ton derrick and winch, *Nicky Nook* cost £100,000 to build. Her name came from the popular picnic-site and beauty-spot high up the River Wyre where the headwater streams flow from the Bleasdale Fells. In 1991 the little work-boat was renamed *Wyre Surveyor*. Photo. by P.Horsley.

Trinity House pilot launch.

Fleetwood has been served by experienced pilots since the early 1800's. The first Morecambe Bay pilot boat to operate here was the Lancaster pilot boat *Guide*. Later a single-mast sailing sloop, *Pursuit*, built at Cowes in 1825, was purchased by Fleetwood pilots in 1852. In 1854 a second pilot cutter *Grace Darling*, built at Peel in the Isle of Man, was bought by Fleetwood pilots and in service for the port. These early vessels were superseded by two large schooners, the *Falcon* built at Glasson Dock in 1894 and the Fleetwood built *Leader* purchased by the pilots in 1897. In recent years Trinity House vessels were in service chartered to the Heysham, Barrow and Fleetwood pilots. The Trinity House launches in service have been No. 12 *Viking*, No. 21 *Vigia* and, pictured here, No. 53 *Argus*. Photo. by P.Horsley.

Chapter 10

Ship Building & Ship Repair

The banks of the River Wyre provided a site for shipbuilding long before the founding of Fleetwood. Small boats were built at Skippool whilst both boats and small merchant sailing vessels were built at Wardleys, the two creeks which together constituted the port of Poulton-le-Fylde. Repair work was also effected for the sailing vessels which used the old port. The barque *Hope*, a 3 masted merchantman built for the Baltic timber trade in 1836, is the largest ship recorded as having been built at Wardleys. *Hope*, a 415 tons barque, was lost at sea in 1862.

Fleetwood's first established shipbuilder was John Gibson, born at Kirkcaldy in 1815 and who arrived at Fleetwood in 1837. When he arrived by steamer from Liverpool, passengers landed by gangplank to the steeply sloping riverbank, there being no staging for the steamers. He may well have been engaged in the building of Sir Peter Hesketh-Fleetwood's four sailing flats recorded as having been built here in 1838 but Shipwright John Gibson joined with Blockmaker James Butcher to form the company of Gibson & Butcher in 1839. At first, work appears to have been repair and refurbishment on vessels using the new port, the first ship known to have been designed and built on the stocks by the company was the *Mary Jane*, a small 36 tons, 52ft (15.85m) sailing flat launched in 1848 for the Ulverston iron trade. The company became firmly established and is said to have built as many as 400 vessels. The company lost its riverside yard and slipway when the Railway Company which owned the site needed to extend Fleetwood Station and the adjoining steamer berths in 1892.

Many well known merchant schooners were built at Fleetwood including the *Richard Warbrick, Sarah Ann Dickenson, Useful, Elizabeth & Ann* and the *Manchester*, but the largest Fleetwood built vessel was the Barquentine *Emily Warbrick*, launched in 1872. Most of the vessels from Gibson's yard were fishing smacks and small prawners. In later years William Stoba, who served his apprenticeship at Gibsons, became their foreman and designer and made the yard famous along the West coast for fast smacks and yachts designed by him.

After the closure of Gibson's yard, William Stoba continued his work at Fleetwood as boatbuilder for James Armour Limited. Other boatbuilders and shipwrights at Fleetwood have included Robert Newton & Sons, established in 1870, Thomas Fisher, and the firm of W. Singleton & Bros., later Hugh Singleton.

When steam trawlers began to operate from Fleetwood in growing numbers, several engineering companies were founded at the port. Principal amongst the new companies was the firm of James Robertson & Sons who were not only ship builders and boilermakers but also early builders of steam lorries. Ship repairing was always carried out by the company but the firm gained world-wide fame as designers and makers of winches and auxiliaries – steam, electric and hydraulic. The Lancashire & Yorkshire Railway Company had an Engineering Department and Machine-shop at Fleetwood from the 1850s which maintained and repaired the fleet of Belfast steamers and the numerous dredgers, hoppers and tugs at the port and the larger Trawler Companies also operated their own engineering departments, shipwrights, riggers etc. Over the years shipping using the port of Fleetwood had available the services of many small independent firms of ropemakers, sailmakers, riggers, engineers and electricians and several large companies such as Marconi Limited had local branches servicing shipping at Fleetwood. Whilst much repair work was effected at the quayside, Fleetwood had a grid-iron on which small vessels could undergo inspection and minor repair and several slipways on which larger ships could be taken from the water. Fleetwood never had the facility of a graving-dock in which large vessels could be dry-berthed.

Emily Warbrick ready for launching on 27th February, 1872.

The barquentine *Emily Warbrick* was the largest ship built at Fleetwood and was eighteen months in building. Built for Messrs. R. Warbrick & Company of Fleetwood, the vessel had a registered tonnage of 167 tons, builders' measure 206.25 tons. Seen here on Gibson's building slip, located roughly where the present Lifeboat and Ferry docks are sited, the vessel displayed a full set of signal flags on the day of her launching and, named by Amy Gibson her builder's daughter, the ship was launched broadside to the river on a 20ft tide.

Re-rigged as a top-sail schooner in the 1880's *Emily Warbrick* remained in commercial service, owned latterly by Reney's at Connahs Quay, until 1934. Converted to be a cruising luxury yacht and renamed *Lost Horizon,* the vessel was destroyed by fire when returning from the West Indies in May, 1938.

A Victorian gentleman's private yacht.

Hecate, a yacht of some 20 tons, was built for Mr. Huntington and Mr. Rowley in 1872, typical of many yachts built at Gibson's yard for the Victorian gentry. Other yachts well known in the North West included *Capri, Playmate, Rambler, Mischief, Imp* and in 1901 perhaps the most noted of all, the William Stoba designed *Zarah* which, re-named *Zulu* in 1905, beat all her contemporaries in yachting events along the West coast. *Zulu* was sold in 1969 and was based in the Mediterranean but later returned to the U.K. and was purchased by an American Naval Officer who took her to the United States on his ship. *Zulu* is reputed to be still sailing out of Charleston, U.S.A.

One of Fleetwood's early trawlers slipped for repairs.

The steam trawler *Laura*, built in Earles shipyard at Hull in 1905 and owned by the Fleetwood Steam Fishing Company, seen here out of the water with her bow open for repair and replating. The 279 gross tons trawler *Laura* came to Fleetwood in February, 1905 as a new vessel and fished out of the port until 1921 when she was sold into Spanish ownership. *Laura* was one of four trawlers which, between them, landed 3000 ten-stone boxes of Hake on 17th July, 1905.

Fleetwood's patent slipway.

Fleetwood's first slipway for ship repairing was located outside the Wyre Dock lock and was approached from the area of the Jubilee Quay, it was in use soon after the building of the enclosed dock and could accommodate only one ship at a time. When the railway and docks passed to the ownership of the L.M.S. Railway in 1923 the first major improvement work undertaken for Fleetwood's dock was to increase repair facilities for ships. The old slipway was redesigned and rebuilt under the the supervision of the L.M.S.Railway's consulting engineers. The rebuilt slipway could accommodate three vessels of up to 600 tons displacement each, at the same time - one on the cradle and two on side berths, one side berth being sited on each side of the slipway. The cradle, traversers and machinery were built at Henderson Engineering's Kings Works in Aberdeen and the improved slipway was brought into use in1929.

In this photograph the *Morecambe Bay* lightship has been drawn up the slipway and then traversed to a side berth. The Lowestoft registerd drifter/trawler *Alcazar* has then been hauled up the central slipway.

Endymion FD62, *Sleaford BN207*, and *Bush FD60*.

The three trawlers are seen here in a photograph taken on 4th. January, 1929 on the first occasion when the rebuilt slipway and traversers were used to accommodate three vessels at the same time.

Vessels on the repair slips in Fleetwood's Fish Dock.

A photograph from 1916 showing the oil-engined wooden-hulled Danish auxiliary schooner *Valkyrien* and the Aberdeen registered trawler *Pembroke Castle* on the slipways. *Pembroke Castle* was owned by the Port St. Mary Fishing, Curing and Ice Company and was later registered at Fleetwood as *FD 340*. Improved over the years and with more powerful winching engines, vessels with a displacement measure of up to 1050 tons could be handled.
The slipways were in constant use into the 1980's and the smaller of the two slipways seen here is still available today

The Fleetwood built Steam Ferry *Wyresdale*.

Built by James Robertson & Sons (Fleetwood) Ltd. The ferry was launched on 18th. June 1924. Pictured here on her maiden voyage on Saturday, 26th.July,1924 the 70 passengers were Members and Officers of the Fleetwood and Preesall Councils and their families together with representatives of James Robertson & Sons. The maiden voyage took the form of a cruise to Heysham and Morecambe.

The building of the ship had been delayed, Robertsons had determined to use a single timber for the keel and the 17.5 metres long baulk of American Elm ordered for the keel was late in arriving at Fleetwood.

Wyresdale, 54 gross tons and 67 feet (20.5m) overall, was licenced to carry 250 passengers. Decked with teak and planked with pitch-pine, this fine little twin-screw steamship had been engined from the builders' own workshops. In 1957 the vessel was scrapped after an engine-room explosion which sadly resulted in the deaths of three men.

The grid-iron.

Showing clearly at low water, the grid-iron was set at right-angles to the Jubilee Quay close by the entrance to the docks. Small vessels were floated over the grid-iron on high water to be exposed for inspection or repair as the tide receded. Receiving attention when this photograph was taken were Fleetwood Corporation's Knott End ferry *Lunevale* and, nearer to the camera, the fishing vessel *Rig*, a Ramsgate registered drifter/trawler with the Fishing No. R139.

The Barrow steam tug *Rampside* coming off the repair slips in 1961.

Seen here with steam up ready to move off as soon as she was safely settled in the waters of the dock, *Rampside*, one of the Barrow Docks tugs, was built as *Empire Fir* in 1946. The trawler up on the adjacent slipway is the *Wyre Revenge,* a 338 gross tons diesel engined trawler built in 1956. The slipways could accommodate vessels of up to 47 metres in length. Photograph by P. Horsley.

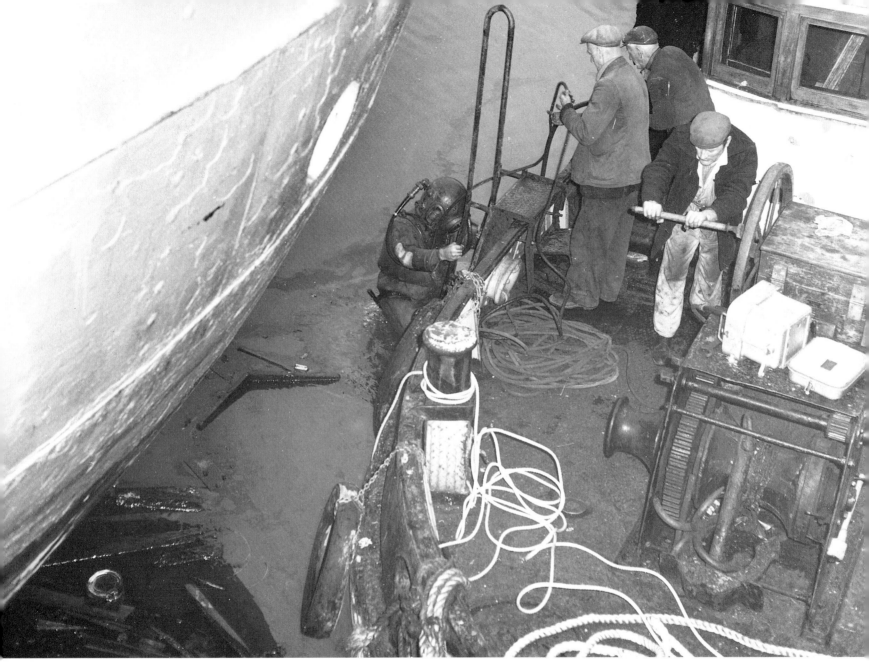

Quayside Work.

A diver prepares to enter the dark, oily waters of the dock to work under the stern of the Hamburg registered coaster *Bernd Wesch*.

A small merchant vessel in Fleetwood for inspection and repair.

The Hull Gates Shipping Company's 790 tons motor coaster *Irishgate* seen at Fleetwood in July, 1967. The vessel, operating for Irish Sea Ferries, was engaged shipping container traffic between Garston and Ireland. Photograph by P. Horsley.

Ship Breaking.

Where Fleetwood's patent 3 berth slipway had been sited just outside the Wyre Dock lock-pit, ship-breaking was undertaken in the 1960's and 70's. Many ships, including Naval vessels, were scrapped. In this photograph the Workington Harbour steam-tug *Solway* (ex *Empire Ann)* awaits the Breaker's torch. Photograph by P. Horsley.

Chapter 11

Visiting Vessels

Over the years since the inception of Fleetwood, a number of ships not normally associated with the port have sailed into the river Wyre. One of the earliest visitations, and probably the most auspicious, was recorded on Monday, 20th. September, 1847 when Queen Victoria, accompanied by the Prince Consort, the Prince of Wales and the Princess Royal, arrived in the Wyre channel at about 3 o'clock in the afternoon on board the Royal Yacht *Victoria & Albert*. Accompanying the Royal Yacht was a squadron of warships comprised of H.M. Ships *Black Eagle, Garland* and *Undine*. The Royal Party, journeying South from Balmoral, disembarked at Fleetwood and continued by train to London.

A visitor to the port 50 years after Queen Victoria's Squadron, and made welcome by the town's fishing community, was the *Euston,* one of the early Mission Ships of the Royal National Mission to Deep Sea Fishermen. *Euston* was a sailing ship built as a smack in 1886 and came to Fleetwood in 1897 to sail as a hospital ship with the "Gamecock" fleet of little steam trawlers owned by Messrs Kelsall Bros. & Beeching which operated at that time from Fleetwood fishing West coast waters and off Ireland.

Prizes of War.

During the 1914-1918 War years Fleetwood was one of the ports used to receive merchant ships caught by the Royal Navy when carrying contraband cargoes to Germany. In the middle distance of this photograph is the 4 masted *Dirigo*, caught with a cargo of oil in drums when attempting to run into a North German port. Brought to Fleetwood, the oil was unloaded from the ship and stored on the open land on the East side of Wyre Dock before being confiscated and used to aid Britain's War-effort.

Several of the Royal Navy's larger vessels have paid visits to Fleetwood but ships of the Fisheries Protection Squadron were regular callers. Very large Naval ships such as H.M.S *Rodney* and H.M.S *King George V,* too large to enter the Wyre, anchored in the Lune Deeps. Tenders from Fleetwood served the vessels and local ferries, tugs and pleasure boats took the public out into the bay to view the big ships. Smaller warships, including submarines, have come into the port over the years and at some time during their visit were often open to the public. The anti-submarine frigate H.M.S *Russell* was one of the last of the Navy's larger ships to visit Fleetwood when on a courtesy visit in 1965.

More recent callers at the port have included all the well known British sail-training ships - *Sir Winston Churchill, Malcolm Miller, Lord Nelson* and the sea cadets' brig *Royalist.* The Paddle Steamer *Waverley* provided a series of excursion sailings from Fleetwood in 1977 which proved very popular with steamer enthusiasts.

Convict Ship.

Seen here in 1910 being towed towards Wyre Dock by the Fleetwood steam tug *Cleveleys* is the old East Indiaman *Success*. The ship was at Fleetwood during a tour of British ports as an exhibition vessel and 'peep-show' attraction. After the British tour the *Success* went to the United States. Advertised as one of the "Felons Fleet" which took convicts to Australia, large placcards on the ship's sides proclaimed.....

"Hell of the Ocean

See the original cells and airless dungeons, the punishment ball, triangle and cat and o'nine tails. See the life-like figures of innocent men transported for life. Everything in its original state, the sight of a lifetime. The world's most remarkable vessel, over 121 years old, raised from the bottom of Sydney Harbour."

However, the *Success* was not a convict ship from the days of 'Botany Bay' nor ever a convicts transport. The teak-built fully rigged 621 tons vessel was launched at Moulmein, Burma, in 1840 and traded to the East Indies. Later she sailed in the Australian emigrant service until 1852 when she was purchased by the Melbourne Authorities and used as a prison ship. Later, in Sydney, the vessel became the lock-up for weekend drunks and seamen deserters. Still in Sydney Harbour, she was later employed as a coal- hulk. The ship's exhibitionist owner was a man of enterprise and imagination, holiday makers from Blackpool flocked to view the ship during her visit to Fleetwood. After a second Fleetwood visit in 1912 *Success* was re-rigged at Glasson Dock for the crossing to America. *Success* survived for many years but was finally destroyed by fire at Port Clinton, Ohio in 1946, a life span of 106 years.

H.M.S. *Fleetwood* arriving in May, 1937.

The Aberdeen class sloop H.M.S. *Fleetwood* was built at Devonport Dock Yard in 1936 and one of her earliest cruises was to the port after which she had been named. Displacing 1060 tons and carrying a ship's company of 100 men, *Fleetwood* was powered by two sets of Parsons turbines which gave a top speed of over 16 knots. Fleetwood served throughout the War as an anti-aircraft escort but in 1946 the ship was later adapted to serve as a Radar Experimental Ship to the Royal Navy Signal School. H.M.S *Fleetwood* was scrapped at Gateshead in 1959.

HMT. *Korab*, Morcambe Bay Examination Vessel during World War II.

The Polish Whaler *Korab* was requisitioned by the Royal Navy in 1940 and then served off Fleetwood as the examination vessel anchored at the edge of the Lune Deeps in Morcambe Bay. In the foreground of this photograph is the little Fleetwood fishing boat *May Baxter,* chartered to the film company making the George Formby comedy "Bell Bottom George" released in 1943 and most of which was filmed at Fleetwood.

The Hunt class Mine Countermeasures vessel H.M.S *Brocklesby*.

Just one of the many small Naval ships which have visited Fleetwood and seen here sailing out of the port after a courtesy visit in April, 1986. *Brocklesby* was built by Vosper Thornycroft in 1982 with a glass-reinforced plastic hull. The ship had a crew of 45 men.

Another small Navy ship, H.M.S *Sheraton*, was a regular caller at Fleetwood and, in recognition of her particular service to the town, the ship was officially 'Adopted' by the District of Wyre Borough. The Ship's crew had been prominent when, at the time of one of her visits, high tides and gales breached the town's sea defences in 1977. Large parts of the town were flooded and many families temporarily homeless, men of the Royal Navy were there to help. Photograph by P. Horsley.

The British Army's landing-craft/supply ship *Ardennes*.

Flying the flag of the Royal Corps of Transport and crewed by soldiers, the ship was photographed leaving Fleetwood on 23rd. May, 1992 after landing four 'Viking Longships'. *Ardennes'* odd cargo had been brought from the Isle of Man for display as a part of the Army's contribution to the pageant of the once every twenty years Preston Guild celebrations.

M.V *Balmoral* ferrying cruise liner passengers to Fleetwood.

Built by Thornycroft & Co. Ltd. in 1949 for the Southhampton / Isle of Wight service, *Balmoral* was chartered to P & A Campbell's Bristol Channel fleet in 1969. During her service with Campbell's "White Funnel" fleet the ship was contracted to act as a tender for the cruise liner *Gripsholm*. Too large to enter ports such as Fleetwood but with visits to Blackpool and to the Lake District featured in the itinerary of the passengers, *Balmoral* ferried *Gripsholm's* tourists to the landing stage at Fleetwood where trams and coaches waited to take the visitors onwards. Photograph by P. Horsley.

The cruise liner *Gripsholm*.

The 1957 built, 23191 gross tons, *Gripsholm* of the Swedish American Line pictured at anchor off the Wyre Light in Morecambe Bay. The ship later became *Navarino* in Greek ownership and then Regency Cruises' *Regent Sea*. In 1996, serving German tour operators, the liner has regained her original name and again sails as *Gripsholm*.
Photograph by P. Horsley.

Chapter 12

Off-Shore Oil and Gas Field Services

During the 1970s and 1980s extensive exploration activity was being carried out in the Irish Sea and in Morecambe Bay in a search for oil and gas reserves. Fleetwood was the base for that exploration work and many vessels connected with the off-shore industry worked out of Fleetwood. Large ocean going tugs such as the 674 gross tons, Rotterdam registered, *Mississippi* came into port after bringing rigs and platforms to work at the new drillings. The port, however, was mostly used by supply ships. These long, low hulled oil-rig supply ships such as the Glasgow registered *Stirling Rock* operated by the Stirling Shipping Company worked out of Fleetwood then and, for several years, vessels of the Smit Lloyd fleet also made Fleetwood their 'home'.

When these off-shore fields began production, the port of Heysham was chosen as the operating base. Supply ships, Anchor Tugs, etc., no longer used Fleetwood. Stand by ships such as those from the East coast based *Brittania Marine* made some use of the Fleetwood facilities from time to time and other Safety and Rescue ships came in occasionally. Many Fleetwood trawlers became Safety vessels at the North Sea off-shore oil-fields.

The port's chief link with the off-shore oil and gas industry is now provided by the Fleetwood Nautical Campus of Blackpool and The Fylde College. Courses for the Survival Certificate required by personnel employed off-shore are offered by the College and the little bright orange coloured survival boats can often be seen bobbing about in the Wyre as the trainees go through their paces.

Fleetwood's Offshore Survival Centre platform.

Housed at the platform, two of the bright orange survival units and the helicoptor cabin are seen here in this photograph, each one playing a different part in the survival training course offered to persons engaged in work on oil and gas offshore rigs. Formerly Fleetwood Nautical College, the Nautical Campus of which the survival platform is a part is now a constituent section of Blackpool and The Fylde College. Offshore survival training courses have been running in Fleetwood since 1983.

Smit Lloyd 3 returning from the drilling area off Blackpool in 1982.

The supply and service ship *Smit Lloyd 3* was one of several 799 gross tons sister ships in the Dutch owned Smit Lloyd fleet operating out of Fleetwood during the early stages in the development of the Morecambe Bay gas fields. None now work out of the port. Photograph by P. Horsley.

The Bremen registered shallow-water survey vessel *Manta*.

Built at Bremerhaven in 1981, this shallow draught vessel could operate in water depths of little over one metre and was specially built for survey work close inshore. The ship, which had been described as an "electronics-packed raft" was brought to carry out survey work in Morecambe Bay when exploratory work both off-shore and on-shore was linked in work to gauge the extent of the reserves in the Bay and under the Over Wyre areas of Lancashire. Photograph by P. Horsley.

Colne Phantom, oil rig safety vessel.

As Fleetwood's trawlers began to be unprofitable after the loss of the Icelandic fishing grounds and the introduction of fishing quotas and restrictions, many fine trawlers found employment as stand-by Safety Vessels in the developing off-shore oil industry. The 431 tons *Boston Phantom FD252*, one of Fleetwood's very successful trawlers, became the Colne Shipping Company's *Colne Phantom* and went off to take up duty at the oil platforms. Photograph by P. Horsley.

Chapter 13

Fleetwood's port
An outline of 150 years of
developments

1835 The first riverside wharf levelled and edged.

1839 Fleetwood created a 'Distinct Port' with Customs House.

1840 The Wyre Channel buoyed and lighted.
Building of enlarged stone quay begun.

1841 Iron-piled quay faced with 7" thick (178mm) iron plating completed.

1844 Customs Board reclassify Fleetwood as a "sub-port" under Preston.

1845 400 yard (365metres) wooden pier for use as a passenger berth built to extend northwards from the Iron Quay.
Sixteen hand-cranes installed along the Quays.
Three-storey Bonded Warehouse built.

1846 A portion of the wooden pier roofed over.
The stone quay southward of the Iron-Quay completed to a length of 1400ft.(427metres) and dredged to give not less than 10ft. of water (2.05metres) at low spring tides.

1849 Fleetwood restored in status to a 'Distinct Port' after having been classed as a sub-port under Preston from 1844.

1850 North End wooden pier improved by alteration to two-deck staging.

1854 Coast Guard Station established at Fleetwood.

1857 Separate warehouse and railway despatch facilities provided for the FishTrade.

1859 Roofed pier at North End enlarged by the addition of a goods shed measuring 190 ft. x 30 ft. (58metres x 9metres). A lifeboat Station established at Fleetwood.

1863 Two steam cranes added to the shore facilities along the quays (more were added over the years).
1000ft. (305 metres) ground chains were fixed in the mid-stream river bed by Mitchell's patent screws and mooring buoys attached. Large ships then moored in safety stem and stern in line with the river channel.

1864 Housing provided for six Coastguards and their officer.

1868 A livestock market established at Fleetwood to handle cattle from Ireland. Prior to this date imported cattle had been sent on by rail to Preston and inland.

1869 Steam ships regularly engaged in the coal trade to Ireland. Coal-Chutes installed for direct loading from railway wagons to the ships.

1871 The Lancashire & Yorkshire Railway Company took over the building of an enclosed dock at Fleetwood after the failure of a private company which had been formed for that purpose.

1875 A warehouse for the storing of imported cotton was erected.

1877 Wyre Dock opened. The 305 metres x 22 metres dock was constructed of Longridge stone capped with coping stones of Cornish granite.
A lock 15.25 metres wide linked the dock to the dock channel and river and a 15 acre timber pond opened from the dock.

1882 Grain Elevator erected at Wyre Dock and in service from 1883.

1883 A large new railway station was built alongside the North End steamer pier and the North End goods shed rebuilt.

1892 The North End pier extended to provide the No.1 berth used by the Isle of Man steamers. Timber-built staging consructed southwards from the stone quay along the West side of the docks channel - this wooden staging took the name 'Jubilee Quay' in 1897 to mark the Diamond Jubilee of Queen Victoria.

1902 Fleetwood's cargo trade greatly declined.
Some steam trawler owners took up space in Wyre Dock and Goods-sheds Nos. 1 & 2 at the dock were converted for use as a Fish Market and fish-sheds. Sailing smacks and some steam trawlers continued to use the riverside quays and the Jubilee Quay.

1908 Work commenced to convert the timber pond, which opened from the Wyre Dock, into a specially designated Fish Dock with its own handling and fish trades facilities. Fylde Ice & Cold Storage Company formed. A coal bunkering facility capable of handling 50tons of coal per hour was erected on the East side of the Fish Dock.

1910 North End staging extended outwards over the river to deeper water and repaired and strengthened. Australian Blue Gum timber was imported specially for this work and unloaded from a large barque anchored at the mid-river 'Canshe Hole' opposite the North End berths, the last large vessel to discharge her cargo at Fleetwood from a mid-river mooring.

1915 New large coaling gantries erected on the Fish Dock coaling berth.

1928 The Belfast Steamer Service transferred from Fleetwood to Heysham.

1940 The daily Isle of Man service transferred from Liverpool to Fleetwood.

1946 The daily Isle of Man service restored to Liverpool. The Fleetwood to Douglas service reverted to summer season sailings only.

1951 The Isle of Man Steam Packet Company erected a 'Lean-to' glass roof canopy along the railway station wall to shelter passengers waiting to board the Isle of Man Steamers.

1952 The Wyre Dock lock pit deepened and the sill lowered to permit the passage of vessels of up to 5.5 metres draught.

1961 The North End steamer berths condemned as being "Beyond economic repair". The Fleetwood - Douglas service closed by the Isle of Man Steam Packet Company.

1963 British Transport Docks Board assume control of the Port of Fleetwood.

1965 Demolition of the wooden North End berths and of the Fleetwood railway station.

1968 A small floating passenger stage was built at the site of the old North End berths for the use of North West Hovercraft Ltd. who proposed to establish a hovercraft service to the Isle of Man.
Messrs Calder & Grandige restart a timber importing trade.

1969 North West Hovercraft Ltd. charter the Norwegian motor vessel *Stella Marina* and restart a Fleetwood - Douglas summer service.

1971 New steel-pile and concrete dredger berth converted to a two-level passenger stage for a renewed Fleetwood - Douglas summer service.

1972 Mayer Newman Limited establish at Wyre Dock facilities for the handling and loading of metal scrap, mainly for export to Spain.
The old wooden Jubilee Quay demolished.

1973 Work completed on a new re-enforced concrete Jubilee Quay.

1975 Link-span roll-on / roll-off vehicle ferry berth constructed at the North End for use by P & O's "Pandoro" ferry service to Ireland. Messrs. Sheard Stubbs (Liverpool) Limited build new grain elevators on Wyre Dock for animal feedstuff imported from European ports.

1976 New fish market Facilities constructed on the Fish Dock.

1982 Associated British Ports Ltd. assume ownership of the port of Fleetwood.

1983 Modern crane system for cargo handling installed on Wyre Dock.

1988 Messrs. Sheard Stubbs end grain import operations at Fleetwood and the grain elevators dismantled.

1989 Scrap metal exports cease.

1990 Conversion of Wyre Dock for development as a yachting marina begins.

1992 Wyre Docks estate cleared to prepare for a "Harbour village" development linked to the Marina.

1993 Fleetwood Fish Dock and Fish Market continues in operation. Work begins to bring the Fish Market buildings and facilities up to the highest European Union standards.

1994 Fish Market facilities and Auctions Hall completed to the latest Euro-Standards.

1995 *Jacinta FD 159* a 615 gross tons stern-trawler gifted to Fleetwood enthusiasts by J. Marr and Son Ltd for restoration and preservation to mark Fleetwood's Maritime heritage. Open to the public in Fleetwood's Fish Dock for conducted tours of the vessel.

In 1839 Liverpool artist William Gavin Herdman (1805-1882) made a series of sketches illustrating what was then Lancashire's brand-new port of Fleetwood. Here, Herdman's sketch shows Queen's Terrace and the original wharf.

The small sailing ships moored at the riverside wharf would safely settle on the mud at low tide but larger vessels moored at the 'Canshe Hole', a natural deep-water pool in mid-river. The little isolated building beyond the moored ships was the Customs Watch-house. The large, detached, porticoed, building in the middle of the terraces of Georgian style houses was Fleetwood's Custom House built in 1838.

The riverside wharf is now occupied by the 'Pandoro' vehicle - ferry berth. All the buildings depicted in the sketch are still in use today. The houses remain as residencies, the Custom House, later Fleetwood's Town Hall, is now the Fleetwood Museum with an excellent maritime collection, and the old Watch-house has become an Ice-cream kiosk.

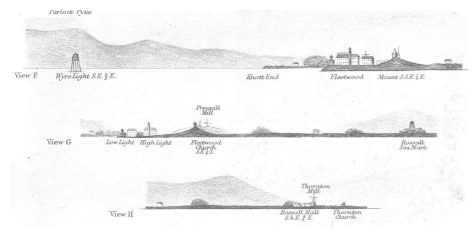

In 1846 Captain Denham, RN. and Commander Williams, RN. charted after detailed survey the Lancashire and Cumbrian coastal waters. Their sketches of the leading marks for the North Fylde and Morecambe Bay coasts were added to the charts for Fleetwood and the Wyre approaches in 1853.

The sketch denoted view F had the note "Wyre light in one with Parlick Pike S.E.2/3E leads through the Swath to Fleetwood".

That denoted view G reads "Preesall Mill opens South of Fleetwood Church S.E.1/4S. clears Fisher Patches".

View H carries the note "Thornton Mill in one with Rossall Hall tower S.b.E.3/4E. clears all the flats in 4 fathoms".

That many of the prominent features so far inland were clearly visible from the sea demonstrates how sparse were the buildings and occupation of the North Fylde in the 1840's. Most of the features shown in the sketches would now be completely hidden by the countless buildings of the district which today crowd close to the shore. Other important features of those years have vanished. Preesall Mill is but a stump, Fleetwood's Parish Church lost its spire, Larkholme Farm (spelt 'Larkham' on Captain Denham's chart) has gone, as has the Rossall Sea Mark which was established at Rossall Point by the Lancaster Harbour Commisioners in 1769.

This print of 1855 views Fleetwood from the Knott End side of the Wyre and many new buildings had appeared in the town during the fifteen years which had passed since Herdman's sketches had been drawn. Small boats are beached at Knott End and in the river three small paddle-steamers are shown. One such vessel registered at Fleetwood at that time was the single-masted, sloop-rigged, wooden hulled paddle steamer *Flying Dutchman* of 26 tons burden, built at Sunderland in1852. This little tug and harbour tender was broken up in 1857. Other small paddle steamers working at Fleetwood at that period were *Nile*, built at Blackwall, London in 1837 and *Cumbria*, built at Paisley in 1845. Much larger two and three masted paddle steamers operating out of Fleetwood at that time were *Fenella, Royal Consort* and *Princess Alice*. Also depicted in this print are large sailing vessels moored in mid-river and the original line of the railway from Preston to Fleetwood, visible as it skirted Fleetwood Marsh on its row of wooden trestles.

Medallion issued to commemorate the opening of Fleetwood's first dock in 1877.

The face of the medallion carries the badge of the Fleetwood Town Board. The reverse represents a three masted sailing ship square rigged on all masts and a railway engine, tender and carriage emphasising the port's role as an integral part of the railway system.

The first vessel to enter the new enclosed dock was the barque *Armstrong* which docked on 8th. October, 1877 with a cargo of timber. Photograph by P. Horsley.

Paddle steamer *Duke of Connaught* at the North End steamer berths.

The P.S. *Duke of Connaught* (1) is seen here alongside the wooden steamer berth which was built in 1845, partly roofed over in 1846, and to which the goods shed was added in 1859. Gas lighting was installed from the outset, 'town' gas being supplied by the Fleetwood Gas Company founded by Sir Peter Hesketh-Fleetwood in 1840. A new railway passenger station was built next to the steamer pier and goods-shed in 1883 and linked to the wooden staging by a covered walk-way. The berths themselves were extended in 1892. Station and steamer berths were demolished in 1965 after the "Beeching Axe" had severed Fleetwood's main-line railway link.

  Built by the Barrow Ship Building Company in 1875, the P.S. *Duke of Connaught* (1) was the first of the Fleetwood - Belfast steamers to bear a 'Ducal' name and started the tradition of the Railway Company 'Dukes'. The ship served on the Belfast route until 1893 then was broken-up and scrapped in Glasgow.

Fleetwood harbour scene, 1880.

Merchant schooners at the stone quayside, a bucket-dredger working at the entrance to the Dock channel and lighters lying in the approach to the locks.

Sailing ships in Fleetwood's Wyre Dock. A photograph believed to date from 1881. Certainly the scene was pictured before 1882, the year in which the building of the port's grain elevator commenced on the site. It is interesting to see how many of the vessels have sails spread, perhaps for drying.

Timber ship unloading in mid-dock.

Baulks of timber and sawn deals have been unloaded into the dock through a hatch or 'port' in the bow of the ship. Once in the water the timbers were then rafted together ready to be floated to the timber pond where they were sorted and readily hauled from the water up the sloping sides of the pond ready for stacking.

Steam ships lie at the quay alongside the grain elevator which is just visible at the right-hand edge of the photograph and thus dating this picture as being after 1883.

Wyre Dock looking southwards from the entrance lock.

A photograph thought to date from 1895. Timber is stacked on the end of the dock and beyond was the timber-pond, the entrance to which is masked in this photograph by the large sailing vessel moored in mid-dock. On the East side of the dock a steam-ship, with masts rigged to carry sail, is discharging to the grain elevator. Tucked in under the stern of the steamer is one of the many merchant schooners which over the years brought their cargoes to the port and took away shipments of coal, salt, dried Cod or salt-fish, some of Fleetwood's most regular outward shipments of those late 1800's. Large vessels, after discharging at Fleetwood, usually left light to pick up export cargoes from Liverpool or Welsh steam coal from the ports of South Wales for shipment to overseas bunkers.

Large sailing vessels held in Wyre Dock at low tide.

The three mast barque riding high and light in the South West corner of the dock is moored close by what was then the entrance to the 15 acre timber pond to which she had, perhaps, just discharged her cargo. In 1908 the pond was converted into the Fleetwood Fish Dock, a task which was not completed until 1911. The small steamer seen in this photograph is the Railway Company's steam lighter *Rossall*, built by the Barrow Shipbuilding Company in 1881 and in service at Fleetwood until 1913.

The vessel on the left of the photograph is a dandy-rigged fishing smack. Leading the mid-stream column is a small steam coaster of the type often termed locally a "steam Flat", a little cargo carrier, many of which worked into the Mersey and along the North West coast. The steamer is followed by a "Jigger Flat", the sail forerunner of the steam Flat but which continued to work from the Mersey, the Weaver and the Dee to the ports and creeks along the coast long after the advent of the steamers. On the right of the photograph is a schooner, one of the two Pilot-schooners which operated out of Fleetwood. The code 2F marking on her mainsail, just discernable in the photograph, identifies her as *Leader* built at Fleetwood in the yard of John Gibson and Sons and fitted out and rigged as a schooner in 1897 for the Fleetwood pilots Messrs. Ball, Edwards, Iddon and MaCall who were registered as the owners of the schooner. *Leader* was sold to a Whitehaven owner in 1921. The port's number 1 pilot schooner was *Falcon*, built at Glasson Dock in 1894 and sold to the Belfast Harbour Commissioners in 1915.

The Dock Channel and the lock giving entry to Wyre Dock viewed from the top of the grain elevator in 1911.

A trawler can be seen in the lock and a cargo ship is berthed at what was then the Timber Quay in the North-East corner of the dock where one of the port's old steam cranes can be seen. Moored abreast of each other on the opposite side are the L & Y Railway's three sand-hoppers *Blackpool, Lytham* and *Kirkham*. For very many years until its demolition at the end of World War II, Peregrine falcons nested on the North East side of the grain elevator roof from where this photograph was taken.

When this aerial photograph was taken in the 1930's, general cargo traffic through Fleetwood had dropped dramatically. The grain elevator of 1882 still stood but had been unused for many years and was eventually bought by the firm of MacFisheries Limited who intended to convert it to be used as a fish processing and packing factory. This conversion scheme came to nothing and the elevator building was finally demolished in 1944. Wyre Dock, built originally as a general cargo dock, is seen here full of trawlers waiting to go out to the fishing grounds. Fleetwood Fish Dock in the forefront of the photograph was bounded on three sides by buildings of the Fish Market and its associated traders, just one corner of these buildings can be seen here.

On the opposite side of the dock is the coaling berth and beyond it the two "Inside" slips can be seen, each occupied by a trawler. In the background of the photograph, beyond the entrance lock, the "outside" slip can be seen with a trawler drawn up out of the water.

Aerial veiw in 1939 looking South over the mouth of the Wyre.

The photograph looks down on Fleetwood's North End steamer berths, the railway station, and on some of the town's earliest streets and buildings. The railway line can be seen curving alongside the docks channel in which one of the old bucket dredgers is at work and beyond, on the West bank of the Wyre, the disused straight line railway embankment of 1840 is clearly visible. Frequently undercut by the tides and by the run of the river, this portion of the Preston & Wyre Railway's track was abandoned in 1856 when the line was curved to the West to avoid the marshlands. The two arms of I.C.I.'s Burn Naze jetty and the old Fleetwood Salt Works and Alkali Plant are visible in the background.

Fleetwood's old North End steamer berths were demolished along with the railway station, goods sheds and riverside buildings. The river bank was re-faced with stone and concrete. In 1971 a new berth was built for the Isle of Man steam Packet Company's newly restored service and here in 1977 *Lady of Mann* (2) is at the berth. Beyond the Steam Packet ship is the former *Stena Timer* still in her Swedish colours at Pandoro's Fleetwood berth which was completed in 1975. *Stena Timer* became Pandoro's *Jaguar*. Photograph by P. Horsley.

Modern grain silos erected at Fleetwood in 1975.

Fleetwood's first grain elevator which features in most early photographs of the port was completed and working from 1883 and had a capacity of over 2800 tons of grain. When it was built it was said to be to "The most modern American standard and to incorporate the latest drying plant, cleaning and handling machinery". The old elevator was sold for use as a fish processing factory in the mid-1930's and demolished in the 1940's. Fleetwood's link with the grain trade was restored in 1975 when Messrs. Sheard Stubbs opened a battery of modern grain silos at the port. The silos, each of which had a capacity of 850 tons, handled animal feed stuff brought largely from Common-Market ports but were dismantled in 1988 after only 13 years service, the last shipment having been discharged to them at the end of 1987. In this photograph taken in June, 1975, the Guernesy registered *Portelet* and the Hamburg registered *Alpha* are at the grain wharf.
Photograph by P. Horsley.

Fleetwood's Wyre Dock Marina, 1996.

Index of ship photographs

Index of ship photographs *(continued ...)*